Trust God
    on your.
        journey

Sara Jane Briggs
Pastor Larry

THE LONG GOODBYE

JOURNEY TO A MIRACLE

SARA JANE BRIGGS

SIR
BRODY

— BOOKS —

DEDICATED

TO YOU, THE SUFFERING, THE BROKENHEARTED
Luke 4:8–19
The blind will see.
Those downtrodden will be freed from oppression.
The time of the Lord's favor has come!

TO YOU, THE CAREGIVER, THE FAMILY, THE PRAYER WARRIOR
Mark 2:2–4
You, who carry the sick and broken to the feet of Jesus.
You, who carry the weight, breaking through barriers to lay
the needs of others before the Great Physician.

TO YOU, DR. KISHOR DABHI, OUR PRIMARY CARE PHYSICIAN
We thank God for your wisdom and encouragement.

TO YOU, OUR SONS, DAUGHTERS-IN-LAW, AND GRANDCHILDREN
Like arrows in the hands of a warrior are our children.
Psalm 127:4
Scott and Amy Briggs
Savannah, Madison, Scott Jr., and Sara
Bryan and Kelly Briggs
Trinity, Gracey, Destiny, and Brayden
Robert and Grey Briggs
River and Ivy

TO YOU
When the day of evil came, you were able to stand your
ground, and after you had done everything to stand,
Larry,
my husband, my love, my hero—you stood.
Ephesians 6:10–13

CONTENTS

FOREWORD

BY GREY BRIGGS

"This was his last Christmas." The words trembled from her lips.

It was a warm, humid summer day—months after Christmas had come and gone. The kids played joyfully outside. They rode their scooters with flushed faces, played basketball, and chased each other in a game of hide-and-go-seek through a small patch of trees beside the house. Papa looked on. I'm sure the kids sensed the tension in the air. We told them a little of what was happening, but as kids do best, they continued to play and love on Papa just the same.

Inside the house, heaviness filled the room. Her words pierced deeply. I can only imagine the thoughts circulating at that moment.

Selfishly, I cried inside. "You can't do this, God!" I knew the feeling all too well—the loss of a father. The sick feeling came back as if my mom was telling me all over again: "Girls, your dad is gone." I looked into Jane's tear-filled eyes, and God showed me how strong she was, and more importantly how strong He is.

Living eight hours away, we were not able to see the progression as slowly and steadily as the rest of the family, so her news was frightening and surreal, but seeing how Papa had drastically changed confirmed her words. Being the daughter-in-law who lived in Tennessee, I felt inadequate when Jane asked me to relay my thoughts on everything that has happened this year, but God showed me that my distance allows me to see the story with clarity.

Let me begin by telling you a little about Larry Briggs, better known to my children as Papa, the magnificently humble man this story is centered around. And let me end by explaining who God graciously called to be not only his caretaker, but also his beacon of faith and his confidant, the strongest woman I know—Jane. Only her words can do this story justice, but she is too humble to speak about herself, so I am cautiously sneaking in the honors.

Since I met Papa more than sixteen years ago, he has always been a humble man, full of faith and integrity. He pastored for many years before becoming a chaplain at a prison. He prayed for the sick and seen them healed on countless occasions. He imparted words of love and wisdom from the pulpit and in his home. He started churches all over the United States.

But the one picture that sticks out to me and will forever resonate in my heart is the image of him immediately leaving the table after dinner to wash the dishes. Trivial as that may sound, I did not grow up with men in my life who were willing to selflessly do the dishes for their family. So the image of Papa clearing the table, even before we had a chance to finish our drinks, will always resonate in my heart as the epitome of a living example of Christ's humility.

This picture is a minuscule glimpse of the life Papa has

led. Seeing him suffer over the years has made me angry and sad and confused. When he didn't know who I was this July, the questions I asked echoed those of most who go through loss and tragedy: "Why? Why him? What has he done to deserve this?" But then I looked at Jane. She wasn't asking why, and she had every right to. After all, he is her husband, her partner in life, the father of her children, the father of my husband, the Papa of my children.

I look to Jane, or Nana as we call her, for too many things to count. She is the pillar that holds her family together, the mom whose knees are worn from nights kneeling in prayer over her sons, husband, students, loved ones, and even those who wronged her. She has led the churches alongside Papa for years. She has led revivals and prayers of healing. She has spoken up for the weak and weary and has fought for her family and church members. She speaks truth into the lives around her, and I'm constantly amazed how faithfully she listens to and hears the word of God.

So when she said, "God showed me that would be his last Christmas," we were listening.

That was last year. One year later, I'm writing this account on Christmas Eve. God's faithfulness and His words to Jane a year ago ring true in the most surprising of ways. As the sun rises tomorrow on Christmas morning, God has shown us all, "The Lord will provide."

I will not take away from the words of Jane, who lived and breathed the story, but want to leave you with the story of Abraham and Isaac as a way to share how sometimes God only gives us glimpses of the whole story.

It is difficult, heart-wrenching, and unbearable at times, but He is constantly growing, changing, and forming us into whom He wants us to be. The refining fire is painful. Being asked to sacrifice your son is unthinkable and unfair. Being asked to trust God when your husband or father is suffering feels like a burden too heavy to carry, but when we submit all that we are to Him, as Abraham did, and as I have continued to see Jane do, He might just surprise us with a sacrificial ram and a lifetime of promises.

God tested Abraham, and said to him, "Abraham!"
And he said, "Here I am."

He said, "Take your son, your only son Isaac, whom you love, and go to the land of Moriah, and offer him there as a burnt offering on one of the mountains of which I shall tell you."

So Abraham rose early in the morning, saddled his donkey, and took two of his young men with him, and his son Isaac. And he cut the wood for the burnt offering and arose and went to the place of which God had told him. On the third day Abraham lifted up his eyes and saw the place from afar. Then Abraham said to his young men, "Stay here with the donkey; I and the boy will go over there and worship and come again to you."

And Abraham took the wood of the burnt offering and laid it on Isaac his son. And he took in his hand the fire and the knife. So they went both of them together. And Isaac said to his father Abraham, "My father!"

And he said, "Here I am, my son."

He said, "Behold, the fire and the wood, but where is the lamb for a burnt offering?"

Abraham said, "God will provide for himself the lamb for a burnt offering, my son." So they went both of them together.

When they came to the place of which God had told

him, Abraham built the altar there and laid the wood in order and bound Isaac his son and laid him on the altar, on top of the wood. Then Abraham reached out his hand and took the knife to slaughter his son. But the angel of the Lord called to him from heaven and said, "Abraham, Abraham!"

And he said, "Here I am."

He said, "Do not lay your hand on the boy or do anything to him, for now I know that you fear God, seeing you have not withheld your son, your only son, from me."

And Abraham lifted up his eyes and looked, and behold, behind him was a ram, caught in a thicket by his horns. And Abraham went and took the ram and offered it up as a burnt offering instead of his son. So Abraham called the name of that place, "The Lord will provide"; as it is said to this day, "On the mount of the Lord it shall be provided." —*Genesis 22:1–14 (ESV)*

The Lord will provide. We have seen His faithfulness firsthand. The tears, the pain, the sorrow, and the fear have been replaced with a sacrificial ram, and His eternal promises ring true this Christmas morning.

INTRODUCTION

"One of the hardest things you will ever do is grieve the loss of a person who is still here." —A. Grace Taylor

Sometimes death comes abruptly and unexpectedly, like a thief, leaving family and friends in shock and disbelief. Hearts crash with emotion, ripped from the foundation by the tornadic details. There are no words of consolation. All you can do is be there.

I've been with those who minute by minute, hour by hour, day after day, stand helplessly by as their loved one struggles against an illness taking them slowly to the valley of the shadow of death.

I dare not say which is hardest—prolonged death or immediate, unexpected passing. Each has its own difficult journey.

My dad died suddenly, in the middle of one of his corny jokes with my mom by his side. No warning. No signs. Mom didn't get to say goodbye. None of us did. He was with us one moment and then, he was gone.

Today our neurologist confirmed what I already sensed. My journey of many long goodbyes to my husband has only just begun. Leaning over the bathroom sink, nauseated with heartbreak, I ask God "Why? Why his mind. The very gifting that he has used for You? Why?"

As those words spill from my lips, something changes. My prayer follows suit.

"What? What may I do to bring glory to You? Thy will be done . . . give us this day our daily bread."

Although I feel so weak that every muscle seems incapable of support, I also feel peace beyond understanding. God has entrusted me to care for His good and faithful servant.

As you walk with me through this journey, I pray it will encourage you to have a deeper faith as you remember that God is greater than all your questions and inadequacies.

PREFACE

It was August 2015. We were in my hometown of Clover, South Carolina, for my mother's funeral. I'd driven that day as Larry didn't feel well. It was the first time I noticed how oddly out of character he was acting.

But I wasn't the only one who noticed. My entire family knew something was wrong.

Losing my mom was the focus, so I tried to brush Larry's oddities off.

I wasn't successful.

The family often joked that Mom loved Larry best, so it was fitting that he conduct her funeral. He did a fine job, but he wasn't himself. When not preaching, he was in his own world, ignoring all of us and closed off to our pain.

I felt Larry was being selfish, and for the first time in our marriage, I was genuinely angry with my husband. The anger began boiling since the moment Larry learned that Mom passed away. He didn't hug me or pray for comfort. Without emotion or compassion, he patted me on the head like a dog.

"Sorry about that," he said.

He acted that way for days and didn't speak a word to any of my siblings at the funeral.

When they asked what was wrong with Larry, I didn't have an answer.

I now know that Larry didn't recognize them that day. He was scared and confused. Looking back, it was a miracle he functioned as well as he did.

It was then, August 2015, that doctors at the University of Virginia (UVA) Medical Center suspect Lewy Body began to attack Larry's brain. Two years later, August 2017, the UVA staff declared him healed. Every time I talk about The Long Goodbye, someone asks about my writing habits, and here is the embarrassing truth.

I don't see myself as a writer. I don't wake up early or stay up late to hammer out story ideas. I don't mull over new plot lines or pay attention to writing trends. In fact, the only thing I wrote for years was a single Christmas card to my mom, Rosalie McCarter. When she passed away in 2015, my writing dropped to zero.

I realize this confession probably isn't good for book sales. But I hope it is good for God's glory.

Because in your hands, you don't hold the work of a writer with decades of experience. You hold the work of someone who loves Jesus and journaled for a very short, very specific time.

Why did I decide to journal if I never write?

Right now, COVID-19 has much of the world practicing social distancing and isolation. When Larry was deteriorating, I quarantined myself, mentally and physically. I very rarely left Larry's side or let others visit. It was too difficult and too confusing.

I relate to those sharing their pain, concerns, and

heartbreak on social media. They need a way to process their isolation. I did too. So I journaled.

For the first time in my life, I grabbed a journal, and I wrote- without being forced to do so by a teacher.

The journaling process wasn't fun. It hurt to write, but it was more painful to keep it inside.

When God gave Larry back, I decided to publish my journal. I wanted something to give to my family and friends as a reminder of God's faithfulness. I wanted to assure them that while miraculous healings don't always occur, our God is powerful, and He cannot be thwarted by anything.

As Larry and I travel, sharing The Long Goodbye, we're often given the honor of praying for others, and we've seen incredible miracles accompany these prayers. Why do we see miracles today? For the same reason that Jesus used the miraculous—to draw people's attention to the miracle of salvation.

So as you read my journal, remember this was not written by a writer. It wasn't even written to be read by others. It's a humble journal, written by a child who is thankful to her Heavenly Father, the Great Physician who cures incurable diseases and raises the dead.

May God bless you as you read *The Long Goodbye*.

Sara Jane Briggs

Was this a long goodbye to Larry's ability
to function independently?
Was it a long goodbye to him?
I didn't know.
But if that was part of God's plan, then
He would provide.
Our Father would provide either way.

FACING LBD

He begins shaking violently. To keep him from falling to the foyer tile floor, I grab him, throwing both of us onto the couch. I'm pinned under him but at least he doesn't hit the floor. I hold him tightly as he cries out, "I'm falling. I'm falling." I hold him firmly, assuring him that he can't fall. I keep whispering, " I have you."

The attack brings such fear of the unknown. I knew he couldn't fall, yet he felt he was going to no matter how tightly I held him or what I said. It is about twenty minutes until I move him completely onto the couch.

I call our son Bryan and an ambulance. It takes all three of the EMS crew to control Larry's violent, total-body flailing. All the while, he keeps asking, "What is happening? What is wrong?" This is the first time I see his eyes fill with fear.

By the time we reach the hospital, Larry is incoherent. His blood pressure and blood sugar are dangerously low. It takes over an hour before the emergency staff get his blood sugar levels to a point where Larry is somewhat alert.

Neurologist Dr. Mudassar Asghar and the ER staff are calm, which helps, but they have no immediate answers. The neurologist disagrees with the diagnosis of TIAs (transient ischemic attacks or mini-strokes), but doesn't know what is happening.

So Larry is admitted again into the hospital for three days—more tests, no answers. In the following weeks, Larry worsens.

Dr. Asghar takes my panicked calls. He even calls without me calling. His concern is obvious and appreciated. He doesn't know what is happening, but he moves methodically and calmly, eliminating possibilities.

NOVEMBER 14, 2016

Our neurologist calls to inform us that test results are ready for review.

He indicates a possible diagnosis but hesitates to give the medical term. Instead, he asks us to repeat some testing to confirm his direction for treatment. His hesitation signals a dire situation.

NOVEMBER 24, 2016: THANKSGIVING

Larry's balance is a big challenge today. He's confused but wants to celebrate Thanksgiving with our family. It's hard for me to make the decision to go or not. Bryan's family is going with us, so maybe we can make it.

We want to go to our oldest son's home for Thanksgiving. Scott's family moved to Suffolk, Virginia, almost two years ago. He and Amy have been my kind, understanding, listening ears. They make every effort to make things seem normal.

Larry is surprised to see Scott, asking if this is his house and wondering when they moved to Virginia. Larry can't walk or move without being carried. Scott purchased him a wheelchair and I watch our sons hoist their father up the porch steps and into the house. The sight of compassion crushes me.

Inside, Larry can scarcely engage in conversation. When he tries, it is all disjointed sentences. When lunch is ready, I prepare his plate. He struggles to pick up his fork and drops food onto his clothes. He is frustrated and embarrassed. I tell him I'll help, that he need not worry. I try to make feeding him seem routine. An impossible feat. I don't look at our children or grandchildren. I can't let our eyes meet. Can't bear exchanging pain-filled, questioning glances.

We leave soon after lunch.

Twenty minutes into the car ride home, Larry turns to me.

"Is this Thanksgiving?" he asks. "Aren't we going to see Scott?"

Gone.

The spinning gray smoke swirls around me, sucks the air from my lungs.

It suffocates me.

> *"If God can afford to lay me aside from active duty and service, surely I should not object."*
> —*J. Hudson Taylor, Missionary to China*

DECEMBER 6, 2016

Today brings another appointment with our neurologist, Dr. Asghar. Larry is very confused and his mobility is not good. If I stabilize his back, he can use the walker. He is in a great deal of pain, and the headache is so severe it impacts his vision, speech, mobility, and understanding. He's experiencing tremors and jerking that last for a few minutes or hours at a time. The doctor suggests it may be restless leg syndrome, but wants to test for seizures.

So Dr. Asghar schedules a four-day hospital stay for testing. We're positive this is a waste of time, yet agree to go. What option do we have?

Larry stays at the hospital and undergoes the tests. The test results show myoclonic seizures.* We're shocked, unsure where this will take us. Dr. Asghar sends us to the University of Virginia (UVA) Medical Center.

*Myoclonic seizures are brief shock-like jerks of a group of muscles. During a myoclonic seizure, the person is usually awake and able to think clearly. (Source: Epilepsy Foundation)

JANUARY 26, 2017

Today is our initial appointment at the University of Virginia Medical Center. As we walk down the massive hallway, I feel a sense of peace and assurance. I know God has led us to the right place.

We are introduced to Dr. Matthew Barrett, our lead neurologist. He has reviewed all the test results and after an examination, he gives us the diagnosis: Lewy Body Dementia with Parkinson's symptoms along with myoclonic seizures. I hear the words for the first time, but nothing seems real. It's too much information to ingest. Dr. Barrett wants more testing before giving an official timeline of the diagnosis.

Larry's symptoms have become so aggressive since November that the medical title attached to his illness has little impact on me. I don't care what they call it. I care about my husband and what is going to happen to him.

The specialists plan a memory exam but say it may be a month or two until they can get it scheduled. We leave the same as we entered, only now we carry the name of an un-invited stranger who has invaded our lives: Lewy Body Dementia.

JANUARY 27, 2017

We are surprised to receive a call from UVA Medical Center telling us they have arranged to move quickly for the memory test. It will be in four days.

JANUARY 31, 2017

Larry is given a four-hour memory test by a team of psychological neurologists, led by Dr. Daniel Brown. Afterward, Larry is exhausted. During the two-hour ride home, he only breaks the silence to say he failed the test.

I assure him it is not a test you pass or fail. It is to formulate a baseline of his memory ability. But I don't believe what I say. Years of teaching and exceptional education training tell me what I say isn't quite true, but it doesn't show in my voice or mannerisms, and Larry relaxes.

We're scheduled to return for results on May 5, 2017—four months from today. I wonder why it takes so long to interpret the results, but I don't mention it to Larry. After all, there's nothing we can do.

I thought the past two years were rough. This is worse by far. These cold winter months reflect the frozen state of my mind.

I'm given websites to research Lewy Body. I only read a few lines before closing the computer. It feels like I am reading material that I shouldn't—forbidden information not meant for my prying eyes.

Larry never asks what I am reading. I never share. I hold my breath each time I open the door of research, trying to understand this horrible illness.

FEBRUARY 15, 2017

It seems our lives are colliding with an enemy determined to destroy us. Larry's attacks are increasing in frequency. What used to occur once every three months and then once a month now happens daily. Hourly.

The side effects vary from days of no sleep to Larry sleeping all day. Balance issues keep me on edge. Larry falls this morning between the bathroom sink and the wall. I try to pick him up, but I can't. Bryan comes. Larry's body is totally limp, but together Bryan and I get him to the recliner.

Bryan leaves and Larry remains awake for hours, for which I'm thankful. I don't want Larry to sleep after falling. He doesn't have any marks, but I want him awake.

He's eating his lunch and watching TV, and I need to take the trash to the curb. He promises to finish eating and not attempt to get up. It takes less than a minute to take the garbage to the end of the driveway, so I'm confident he'll be safe.

When I reach the curb, a tremendous crash sounds from inside the house. I run, my minding scrambling for what could have happened in such a brief moment. I rush in to find Larry again on the floor. This time, he's hurt. He fell into a large bookcase and hit it with such force the sides of the bookcase are splintered from the shelves. Books are scattered and torn.

He struggles against me, trying to get up on his own. I beg him to stop and let me help him, but he keeps on as if he can't hear me. Begging, almost yelling, I try forcing him to stop. He finally submits when I say he's hurting me. I help

Larry crawl to the edge of the recliner, and Larry helps as I pull him onto the chair. He has a bump on his head and a few minor cuts from the splinters of wood.

He says he thought he could get up on his own. He doesn't remember our conversation not to get up. I am scared and frustrated. My friend, Cathy Kaufman, a nurse, comes to check on Larry. She reminds me that Larry can't process or retain conversations.

MARCH 2017: THE MONTH OF TESTING

UVA Medical Center orders more tests: CAT scan, MRI, blood tests, and another spinal. I question the need for more testing only to hear the medical team has to make sure we are actually where they think we are on this journey.

We try to be normal, which is exhausting.

Larry becomes more and more distant. I don't think he understands why we are in and out of doctors' offices. I'm not sure I do either.

Due to Larry's inability to comprehend, I'm allowed to stay with him throughout the testing.

March brings an end to medical tests and begins a deeper, more painful month. I tell myself winter is ending and spring is around the corner, trusting for new life to blossom.

APRIL 3, 2017

I often walk softly to our home's entry foyer to catch a glimpse of Larry sitting alone on the front porch. He never liked sitting outside. Now, it is his secret place with God. His prayer closet.

He can no longer read, but he holds his Bible. Years of studying God's Word, hiding it in his heart, will hold him. He moves his hands tenderly across the surface of the scripture, as if written in braille. He lovingly touches each line and looks to the sky, lost in thought. I don't have to speculate what he's thinking and praying. I know.

Days blend into weeks, weeks into months, and months into years. I can't reflect on recent times without immense pain. I look back at Larry's years of tireless service. The very thought weakens my entire body. Yet, all of this is God's will, His perfect will being done.

APRIL 9, 2017

Bryan, Kelly, and the grandchildren are here for our usual Sunday lunch. Larry feels more comfortable eating in our home office than at the table with the family. Bryan usually joins him for father-son time. Today is different. Brayden, who's five years old, wants to eat with Papa. He sits with Larry instead of running around and playing. Brayden ask if he and Papa can go for a walk together. Larry's balance is cautiously stable, so we help him down the steps of the front porch. Brayden walks slowly beside Papa. They talk as they walk on their short venture. After they walk just two houses down from ours, they turn around and walk back.

After Bryan's family leaves, Larry tells me about their conversation.

Brayden said, "Papa, don't worry about forgetting me. If you forget, I'll just keep telling you my name."

Larry repeats the conversation several times to me, so I wonder if he is confused. I don't know if Bryan and Kelly have told the children about Larry's health, with the possible loss of recognition and names. While Larry rests, I call Bryan to ask if he has talked with the children. He confirms that he has talked to them, explaining to each child according to his or her ability to understand. Bryan calls Brayden to the phone, asking him about his talk with Papa.

"Yes," Braden says, "I don't want Papa to worry about forgetting me. I'll just say, 'Papa, I'm Brayden.'" Then he runs off to play, like a five-year old should.

Larry and I are beyond blessed with ten incredible grandchildren. Now, when Larry and I speak of them, it is to rehearse their names and to whom they belong. I keep family photos nearby, secretly calling the home office his memory room. He recognizes the pictures sometimes, but not often. Tears come to his eyes, as he tells me he's concerned he'll forget River and Ivy, the children of our youngest son, Robert, and his wife, Grey. We don't see them often as they live in Cleveland, Tennessee, so I often show Larry their pictures. Like Brayden's sweet advice, if Larry forgets, I'll just keep telling him.

I wish it was that simple, but it's not. And the knowledge crushes me. However, I trust our memory room will keep their names and faces recorded in Larry's heart, as well as his mind.

When Larry seems lost, I tell him, "Once I get you to your room, you'll be okay." It brings him peace.

The idea of a memory room came from reading the account of a woman trying to explain her challenges with Alzheimer's. She said her life is like a bookshelf. The books on the top shelf are her past, the middle is the present, while the bottom shelf holds her hopes and dreams for things yet to come. The bookshelf represents her mind—clean and in order. Suddenly, a violent shake causes the bookcase and all its contents to plummet to the floor. Books scatter. Pages tear. Try as she may, it is impossible to put the books of her life back in order.

Those are the days when the fog sets in, covering her

mind. She's unable to function, to think, to do, to be. Larry says the same to me as he struggles to help me understand his thought process.

The day Larry fell, breaking the bookcase, was a living example. The books scattered across the office floor were priceless biblical studies we had sacrificed over the years to purchase. Notebooks ripped apart contained his written messages from years of preaching. Seeing them scattered, pages ripped and torn, seemed to predict what we were experiencing and even more frightening, what could be ahead of us.

MID-APRIL 2017

I've given lots of thought to these recent attacks. Do I record the good moments along with the times of confusion, pain, and loss? The latter now outweigh the moments of clarity and light. Yet the hard times make the good moments all the more sweet. So I choose to ramble. *Whatever,* as my granddaughter Trinity says.

APRIL 24, 2017

Larry has always been good with dates. He's the first to remember our anniversary—the date and how many years we're celebrating. I always have to pause and think about dates.

Most of Larry's questions come while I'm driving. I've come to appreciate dark sunglasses and the need to keep my eyes on the road and not glance his way when the pain-filled questions come.

"How long have we been married?"

The pit in my stomach causes me to hold my breath, waiting for the next question. There's always another question. And then another. But he wants the answer to this question.

"Forty-five years," I say. "But you always count a year ahead, so forty-six."

I answer honestly, hoping nothing else will follow, but there is always more.

"Are we happy?" he asks with the empty eyes and monotone voice that is now his norm. "Have we been happily married?"

God holds my heart as I try to joke back. Larry no longer understands jokes, but the joke is my way of making the situation lighter. For me at least.

"Yes," I say. "We are happy. We faced life's challenges together. You and I...we are happy."

He starts to say more, but I don't let him. I move to another topic. He accepts the change. I do, too.

APRIL 29, 2017

This morning, an awful trick comes. It's come before, but I recognize it now.

Larry is present. He acts normal, but unless there is a miracle, it's a brief visit. I'll take what I can get, but when he leaves, the pain and tears will flow. Goodbyes hurt more each time my husband leaves. But for now, for however long, I'll accept it.

We sit together on the front porch, speaking little. There's a gentle breeze, warm sunshine, and birds happily singing. Bethel Worship plays through our Echo speaker.

Larry drinks coffee. I sip a glass of tea. A neighbor rides by on her bicycle. We wave and return to our thoughts. My overcharged, scattered mind races back and forth. A zillion disconnected, short-circuited thoughts scream at me.

Don't think, Jane. Don't. I tell myself this over and over but can't heed the words.

Then Larry says what we're both thinking. "Is this real, Jane? I can't comprehend what this all means."

I can't comprehend it either. Suspect we never will. I try to prepare for the unknown, those things predicted to come. Larry's diagnosis hasn't officially come, yet the doctor's gentle, coded suggestions help formulate an unspoken dread.

I continue researching on my own, feeding the dread.

MAY 5, 2017: UNIVERSITY OF VIRGINIA MEDICAL CENTER

The summation of Larry's test is discussed. The diagnosis of Lewy Body Dementia (LBD) had only been suggested until today. Now, packed tight in an official-looking folder, it rests in my lap.

I sit in the backseat, while Bryan drives. I stare at the folder as if it's a bomb. If I move or flinch, it will explode.

Dr. Brown, our neuropsychologist, explains that LBD isn't normally identified while the patient is living. Typically, it's not until the end that doctors identify LBD.

The end? This isn't the end? There's more?

Dr. Brown calmly, kindly, and clearly shares what the end will be like, and he tells us that the end is closer than we thought. He says LBD usually runs its course in two and a half years, and the last six months are extremely aggressive.

November 2016—six months ago—marked the beginning of Larry's last six months alive.

"You most likely have about two weeks to get everything in order," Dr. Brown states. "If [Larry] wants to have input into end-of-life decisions, this is the time frame."

I feel how hard it is for Dr. Brown to spread these facts before us. I've already learned how to be factual, but I have more to learn.

Dr. Brown says he knows our faith will support us during

these next few weeks. I know it, too.

The ride home is painfully silent, broken only by the revolving question that Larry, Bryan, and I take turns asking: "Are you okay?" Each time, someone blankly replies, "Yes."

I finally break the cycle.

"We're okay and we're not okay," I say. "We're going to continue each day like we have to this point. Live. Do. Continue. Now, let's eat lunch."

The answer brings the spinning to a stop. We stop at a small mom-and-pop barbecue restaurant. There's a long line and standing room only for customers.

As we enter, a customer hands us a menu and offers to let us in front of him. Another gives up his seat for us.

By now, such responses to Larry are so normal that I don't have an option but to accept the kindness of strangers. I offer my gratitude with whispered thank-yous and hope they see the thankfulness pouring from my heart through my tearful eyes. Surely they feel it. They have to see the pain that walking causes Larry, his blank facial expression, and perhaps even my heart breaking as I help him enter the room. Otherwise, why would a room of strangers be so kind?

The struggle to stay normal is causing my head to explode. My temples pulsate.

As we sit down to eat, tears slide down my face before I even know I'm crying. How can I cry and not know it?

Inside, two emotions clash.

1. I must stay strong—Stand up, get done what has to be done.

2. But I'm so weak and lost—Oh, God, this can't be real!

...

MAY 10, 2017

Within a matter of seconds, I'm catapulted from the fog of not being sure this is real to the gut-wrenching reality that it is indeed real. Painfully real. Despite this, I know God can do more than I can even ask or think. And through it all, our trust in Him has not wavered. It has become more steadfast and stubborn.

MAY 14, 2017

"There is no pit so deep that God's love is not deeper still."
—Corrie ten Boom

Nine days ago, doctors suggested Larry would be mentally capable of making end-of-life decisions for about two more weeks. They were correct. We had slightly more than a week. I cannot bear to write more.

MAY 23, 2017

"The loneliest moment in someone's life is when they are watching their whole world fall apart and all they can do is stare blankly." —*F. Scott Fitzgerald,* The Great Gatsby

MAY 24, 2017

Today is Larry's birthday. We briefly attend a meeting with Destination Church staff. They made Larry a birthday cake. The remainder of the day we rest quietly. Larry is lost and confused.

...

MAY 25, 2017

It's early in the morning—dark outside and inside my mind. It's too much to deal with today, so I choose not to think. I choose to be satisfied with knowing His Word says that He will never leave nor forsake me.

MAY 26, 2017

F. Scott Fitzgerald's quote from a few days ago comes to life through the sweet voice of an amazing woman, Jeanne. Sam and Jeanne were pastors in Atlanta in 1976, the same time Larry and I were pastors in Hinesville, Georgia. That's an age-revealing fact. Sam was an admired senior pastor and Jeanne was a nationwide youth pastor mentor.

Our son Bryan met Jeanne and Sam in 2007 at a youth pastor training seminar in Atlanta. Bryan has stayed in contact with them over the past eleven years, visiting several times. When he went to Atlanta to speak at their son's church this month, it had been about four years since he had seen Sam and Jeanne. The visit was eye-opening.

Sam was diagnosed with Lewy Body with Parkinson's two years earlier, and seeing the change in him was painful. Jeanne occasionally called me after Sam's diagnosis, and though I wanted to hear from her, I dreaded our talks. Little did Jeanne and I know that Lewy Body would enter my home as well.

"Jane," she asked me soon after Sam's diagnosis, "have you ever heard of Lewy Body Dementia with Parkinson's?"

I hadn't. But that's all changed. Today, the question has changed, and it takes my breath away.

"Did you ever think we'd be brought into this dreadful club?" Jeanne asks. "There are only a few names on the membership roll. You'll hear people say they know someone with this. No they don't." She speaks with a disappointing anger that mirrors my own. "Do you know how rare this is, Jane?" she continues. "Do you understand the quick loss and results? The disease has a span of about two and half years, with the last six months becoming unbelievably aggressive."

I can't breathe. Sam is a few steps ahead of us, a few months deeper into the disease progression. But it really doesn't matter if the difference is a month or a day. We are both unwilling members.

We don't know anyone else with the disease, but there are others. That's why our neurologist sent us to UVA Medical Center. No one in our area specializes in this rare form of dementia—not one person in all of Richmond. That was my first clue that I was about to face a frightening stranger.

I cherish Jeanne's willingness to reach out to me, to help prepare me, to validate what I'm feeling and the many questions she knew I would have. I weep as my heart breaks for Jeanne and all she's facing with the love of her life. She calls Sam her hero. I can identify. She reveals the challenges of twenty-four-hour care and physical and mental challenges. Jeanne opens her heart as she discusses delusional behavior. But even the word "delusional" sounds benign compared to the ugliness of its truth. Dreams, dreadful dreams don't end when Larry wakes up. Those dreams become the reality of the day. He wakes up but is unable to dismiss the fear of what he continues to see. Because the dream is no longer a dream. It's real. It can be seen and heard and felt.

Our conversation leads me to understand that Larry's disease may be at the same place as Sam's. The distance between them is not identifiable as I initially thought. Jeanne speaks tenderly, yet truthfully to prepare me for what lies ahead.

At this point, I stop reading about Lewy Body Dementia

with Parkinson's and seizures. I've learned enough. The last time I researched the disease, I asked online if anyone had ever recovered.

The answer: No.

Sam's battle ends a few days after my phone call with Jeanne, and heaven gains a beloved hero. Now, my prayers continue for his loving wife, partner in ministry, caregiver, and greatest supporter. I think of Jeanne often. I owe her a debt of love.

It's like a thousand-piece puzzle of blues and grays thrown into a pile. I don't know what the finished picture is supposed to look like or if the pieces even belong to the same puzzle. Each loss, every symptom confirms everything the doctors said. Larry spins from sudden improvement to growing worse. The truth of what Larry is going through hits me like jagged cut glass, piece by piece, a thousand jabs cutting me slightly, deeply, repeatedly. I look at the bleeding and feel nothing. The feeling of nothing is the cut that finally makes me cry.

MAY 28, 2017: MEMORIAL DAY WEEKEND

Robert and his family are visiting from Tennessee. Larry insists on going to church. It's difficult to say no. When the boys and their families visit, Larry pulls his strength together to be present, to be as aware as possible. So how can I say no to the only thing Larry requests of me?

We make it to our seats with little stress. I scan our row of seats, thanking God for the blessing of sitting in His house with Robert, Grey, and their two children. Grey sits next to me. For a few brief moments, life is normal, like it was for so long. Larry's voice calls me back to my new normal.

"Who is that sitting beside you? Is that Grey?"

I nod and my eyes meet Grey's. We exchange glances mixed with support and horrible concern.

"Is that Grey?" he asks repetitively. "Is that Grey?"

As the service opens, he stops the cycling question and listens intently to the singing and the message. Larry struggles visibly to stay connected to reality, fighting the fog of confusion. As church ends, he prays over a man and his wife with complete clarity and sensitivity.

As I assist him to the car, I mention the person we prayed for. He doesn't know what I'm talking about. Then it clicks for me. When people leave Larry's sight, they're gone from his memory. It's like writing on the sand at the beach. When the wave comes, it takes away what was written. The surface becomes blank, waiting for the next imprint and the subsequent wave that will take it away.

While not always recognizable, home is usually our safe place. After lunch, Larry and Robert watch television while the grandchildren play and Grey and I chat in the living room. Larry's balance improves after a short rest. I listen to him talk with Robert when—without notice—clarity is gone.

Larry walks into the living room. "Where are we?" Larry asks. "Is this our home? Are we renting or do we own it?"

I give straight answers and glance at Grey, taking strength from her sweet face.

I breathe and try to move on, hoping that nothing more is revealed while Robert and Grey are here.

God graciously provides His daily bread, strength for the day. It's more than enough.

Robert and Grey are here for a family meeting. It's hard on each family in different ways. I understand each son's perspective. I clearly understand how hard it is to be the sibling who lives out of town. Ministry always meant I couldn't be home for holidays or day-to-day contact with family. I am concerned about how hard it is for Robert's family to see the drastic changes since they can only visit every few months. This visit will be the hardest to date, I'm sure.

It's a typical hot, humid Virginia afternoon. Our ten grandchildren play in the yard, bringing a sense of peace and normalcy mixed with sadness. Sad that Larry can only watch. I search his expression wondering if he knows what's happening. Does he know who they are? Is he silently practicing their names? As he observes the children playing, I meet with our three sons and their wives. It's crushing to see the pain in their hearts. Yet, now is the time to come clean regarding our day-to-day challenges. I can't put it off any longer. I'm running out of time to protect them from knowing everything.

I share my plans, insist I won't seek an extended care facility unless I can't keep their dad safe. I don't believe that will ever be necessary. I leave the conversation open for each to express their thoughts and ask me questions.

The pain-filled room becomes more suffocating than the hot summer day.

I tell them how God prepared me last December for what was coming concerning Larry's health. They hate hearing my words, but they know me. They know I'm telling the truth.

The picture of the six loves of my life, crushed and heartbroken, is forever seared in my mind. It's not necessary to journal our discussion. I can't forget that pain. The force of it is sickening and indescribable anyway.

JUNE 3, 2017

Today marks the last time I'll take Larry to the grocery store. When we leave home, his mobility is stable. I only need two items, and I can be in and out in a few minutes. However,

Larry loses his mobility as we walk down the first aisle. It is so painful watching him try to make it. It comes suddenly, the inability to walk.

I think I'll make it easy and have him wait for me at the front, while I make a mad dash to the dairy department. I'm only gone for a few minutes. When I find him standing at the end of the aisle, I know it—he's lost. Afraid. Gone.

A customer found Larry and stationed him to the end of the aisle, hoping someone will find him or that Larry will recognize who brought him to the store. Once he sees me, relief floods his face. I struggle to get him into the car, afraid I won't be able to keep him from falling. How can his eyes be so blank and empty, yet filled to capacity with confusion?

I keep telling him that he is safe now. I assure him everything will be better once I get him into his home office—his memory room. I am so thankful to have us both safely seated in the car. I give a silent prayer of thankfulness as I pull onto the highway.

Larry calms down, but that's the trap, the deception of Lewy Body. As if a switch flips, Larry goes quiet and barely moves.

"I want to ask you something," he says, "and please tell me the truth." His voice is expressionless.

I hope that maybe, just maybe this once he will ask where we live or where we are going. *Please make it simple*, I silently beg.

"I know you went to see a lawyer," Larry says. "Are you divorcing me? If you are, I understand. This has be harder on you than me. I know you'd be better off. I'm sad, but I understand." He begins to cry.

I can barely catch my breath, let alone answer him. I feel my body melt and plummet to the floorboard. *Focus!* I demand of myself. *You're driving!*

In that moment, God comes to my rescue and gives me His calming peace. I remind Larry that we both went to see the lawyer to make sure our will and other documents are in order. He remembers that, but noticed that I talked to the lawyer privately and suspects I told him I wanted a divorce. That's the way this puzzle keeps breaking apart: truth saturated with confusion.

It's like a gray puff of smoke. Each time he forgets, whether the smallest memory or a huge chunk of our lives, they evaporate the same—with a puff. When did the memory really leave? Am I just seeing the effects of its evaporation? Was it gone days ago? Am I only now seeing the residue of its escape?

JUNE 4, 2017

Today is Sunday, another evaporation of memory. Despite this, it is one of our good days. Larry can walk today with only my arm assisting him. We go to church. Larry recognizes his friend Bill Sanders, who greets us at the church doors. I feel normal for a moment. A brief moment.

Before we make it to our seats, we see Bill again. Larry doesn't know him. Longtime friends, yet their relationship is as good as gone. As we take our seats, any previous clarity is overshadowed by a heavy fog. With each person we pass, there's no recognition.

Then there is our family. I'm sure even with today's evaporation, family will stay. The gray smoldering ashes surely can't burn across the boundaries of our family's love.

We settle into our seats when a sweet couple greets Larry. We've known the Gordons longer than thirty years. They moved to Virginia from Hinesville, Georgia, and even attended the church we pastored in Georgia.

"Good morning, Pastor Briggs," they say in unison.

Larry is instantly upset. He asks me to tell the couple to forgive him as he doesn't know them. He then asks me a series of confusing questions: "Am I a pastor? I thought Bryan was the pastor. Why did they tell me to say hello to Bryan? Where are we? Who are all these people?"

Loss looks me in the face. In one puff of evaporation, gone is a lifetime of ministry. Being a pastor is Larry's identity. His life is caring for God's people. How did it all leave him? When? There are no answers. Only ashes.

JUNE 5, 2017

It's a beautiful day. The sun is shining. I'm hoping a ride will help us both feel better. The sky is a comforting, calm blue and with the windows down, the fresh air makes me feel free.

Larry seems relaxed and at peace, glancing out the car window into the sky. Then he asks if there is some place he needs to be or someone he is supposed to meet. Occasionally, something inside Larry reminds him that his schedule was normally filled with meetings. I tell him he doesn't have any appointments today. That he should just enjoy the day. That it's his day off. But he doesn't relent, asking question after question about the day's schedule. I suspect the demands of his previous, normal life are flashing back to his memory.

I decide to encourage Larry. I tell him that people love to hear him preach. They appreciate his tireless hours of counseling, his love for police officers, and his willingness to help others in need.

He listens quietly, taking in what I tell him. "Am I dying?" he asks. "Is that why people tell me about the good things I've done? Are they making it up so I'll feel better?"

I gather myself to say we are all telling the truth.

"Am I dying?" he repeats. "Is this illness killing me?"

"All our days are in God's hands," I respond truthfully. "We are both safe in Him."

I keep driving and we pass the regional jail. After establishing the chaplain ministry at the jail, Larry was on staff there for ten years. He comments about the size of the building.

I tell him its purpose and that he was the facility's first chaplain. "I did that?" His voice is lifeless.

His comments cause me to realize I'm still adjusting to the loss of the past. Sometimes, even if just for a minute out of the day, he remembers something and I think he's doing better. With this illness, it's one step forward, three steps back; two steps forward, one step back; and then—then, it's gone. Like an electrical short, the light flickers on, off, on, off, on, and then off forever. When I speak of the past, it's as if I'm telling him about someone he doesn't know. So I decide not to tell him of the unfamiliar past any longer. And all past is potentially unfamiliar.

This will be the last time I reference his past work as a pastor, family counselor, chaplain for the police department, jail minister. It's too painful for us both. There's no point anyway. It's just part of this breathless goodbye.

The emptiness of Larry's eyes is what I notice most about his face. His facial muscle tone is gone, adding to his loss of expression. A result of Parkinson's, I'm told. Part of the process. The process. There should be a better word for such loss. Yet, it is God's mercy and grace that Larry remains a gentle soul. That's immeasurable to me.

I'm told he'll become combative. I ask God for mercy.

Mercy can keep Larry from a combative attitude and give me strength to walk through it should it come. I trust Him.

I answer Larry's text messages for him. Through the years, we have done most counseling sessions together, so I know what is needed. My heart breaks when I start referring counseling sessions to other staff members. I know the staff is capable to take over our appointments, but Larry and I are passionate about serving those who come to us in need. This further removes us from whom we are and what God has called us to do. It's one of the saddest parts of saying good-bye to our forty-six years in ministry.

There should be some pause, a warning sound, some notice that Larry is slipping away. Instead, the world passes us by in silence, unaware of the loss of such a great man.

The thought runs through my head, despite knowing it's not true. Many people deeply care, but most days I can't shake off the loneliness. Therefore, I'll give my thoughts to others today. I choose to step outside my situation and pray for them. I can only imagine how others must feel when they lose someone. How does life go on seemingly unaffected by such loss?

I pray for my friend Sherry Zauner. Suddenly, without a moment's notice, her husband, John, entered heaven. He was teaching. It was immediate, yet John was doing what he had always done: helping others be successful like himself. I remember Sherry at the funeral. Was it her nursing skills that kept her focused? Was it her calm, taking-care-of-everyone-else character that kicked in? I know God is her strength, yet how does she face each day without John?

She messaged me one day: "Life goes on and sometimes you think you won't be able to take one more breath, but God is faithful and your friends are here. Lean on them. Lean on

44

me. Be angry, cry, scream, and shout, but don't walk away because He will literally be the only thing that keeps you from falling off the edge. I am here day or night. Call and I will be there."

I knew God would hold Sherry as she processed the loss of her husband, and I know He is holding me. Where else would we go? There's nowhere else to go, no other place I'd want to run and shelter.

People come by. I try to limit whom and for how long. I know they come out of respect and love, yet I don't think it's good for Larry. People tell me to call when needed. They're sincere. Absolutely sincere. Oh, how I wish they could help! But my thoughts and emotions are a priceless perfume, a perfume I can't let spill out. If I open up even the least amount, this perfume would flood out with such volume and force no one could handle it. So I don't. I keep it bottled up instead.

It's strange that even family can't be on the same page. They're busy. They have their own lives. I get it, and I know it's meant to be this way. Yet I'm always excited when they come to visit. Selfishly, it gives me more eyes to watch Larry while I take care of daily tasks. It gives me a safe place to catch my breath, and I cry when they leave. But now, I'm anxious for their departure. I fear they may see how bad Larry's condition, our life together, really is. God has been gracious to shield my loved ones from much of the worst of this whole thing. I don't want the memories, the images, the heartbreak burned into their hearts like it has mine. I'm the spouse. It's meant to be different. I want them to see their dad as strong, healthy, wise, and loving them.

Years ago, on the way to my dad's funeral, mom said, "Losing your dad is not the same as losing your husband." I don't know what made her say it. Maybe one of my siblings said something. Probably tried to say the right thing, but as usual in these situations, it was wrong.

People mean well. I've become increasingly aware of well-meaning statements. They don't offend me. These people who know us and love us are desperately searching for words of encouragement. And they often come out the wrong way. I'm sure I've done the same, and I plan to be more careful.

Nonetheless, what do I want—for them to join me in the watch? No! What they see as glimpses are already too painful. I don't want them to witness it moment upon moment, day upon day. It's too much, and it's not their burden.

My thoughts today center around our faithful friends. There are so many carrying their heavy burdens, too, yet in the midst of their own needs they care about us. Mercifully, they limit their phone calls so I don't have to repeat the same update over and over. I dread that, so I'm thankful for their consideration. I know they care and are carrying us to God daily. Without a word, they greet me with a hug and an exchange of "I'm with you" in their glances. Their silence is well heard by my heart. Although I don't record their names, they are my greatest source of strength. I pray for your needs, friends. Praying for you gives me strength to move onward.

I'm so thankful for the four men who take turns sitting with Larry when I need to take care of business outside of our home. I trust you with Larry at the most crucial times. You are beyond generous and kind.

Others are faithful and timely when they call or text. My precious high school friend Diane Wray reaches out as I do with her. We've been best friends since seventh grade, and her husband recently passed away from cancer. Even in her pain, she speaks love and peace to me. I can't express what her love means to me.

My sister Mary Jo texts or calls almost every day. It's a safe time to cry, to be encouraged. Sometimes we share sweet stories about our grandchildren in order to think about something else. Mary Jo's daughter-in-law Jae-Won sent me a video of her three-year-old son, John-William, praying for Uncle Larry. I play it often. I know John-William's prayer touches the heart of God. It does mine as well.

My sister Jean has such a big heart and is so supportive. She updates my siblings, keeping me from the constant repetition. She tells me Larry is going to be healed. She believes it will happen soon. She insists it will happen by Father's Day, but if not then, by Thanksgiving. I let Jean carry us, not allowing myself to think how this long goodbye will proceed—whether Larry recovers or not. Through God's goodness radiating from Jean and others, we are given strength to face each day that comes. I just trust Him.

Diane Grover understands pain, too. A steadfast child of God, she remains faithful through the toughest of times. She's a friend who understands without me expressing any words. Diane and I are true sisters.

A.J. Ressler is my encourager. She is the iron that sharpens my iron. When I am weak, she sharpens me into strength.

Angela Jennings texts most days. I think of her as my little sister. I know she struggles finding the right words to say. There are no right words. Her love is all I need.

Lanelle Cooper texts or calls daily. She usually texts because she knows that frees me to answer when I'm available. Our families have been united in heart since our sons were toddlers. I know she and her husband, JC, carry us to God daily. What would I do without them?

Larry's step-sister, Gloria Nowling, is priceless. She's a

retired nurse and is helping me understand so much. Her love and wisdom bring me more comfort than I can express.

Then there's our friend Jane Lanham. I can't write her name without smiling. She's my adventure-loving, beach-going partner. She loves us as we do her. Jane's sacrifice of love and prayers are immeasurable. She recently sent me a note. "I'm willing to sit on your front porch all day," she wrote, "waiting to be summoned for a task." I absolutely know she means it.

I saved a text from Melissa Ebert, giving me her love, prayers, and God's unfailing word. "You're witnessing first-hand what the rust and moths of the world eat away," she wrote. "You're also walking out the 'Thy-will-be-done' concept that Christians say we want. The reality of it can be so harsh to our human mind and soul. But I see step by step the Holy Spirit guiding you. The process is terrifying, gut wrenching, and beautiful all at the same time." I haven't shared with Melissa my commitment to the Lord's Prayer: "Thy Kingdom come. Thy will be done. Give us this day our daily bread." Yet she describes perfectly a morning I stood over the bathroom sink, submitting to His will, regardless of what His will meant for Larry and me. Melissa, I'll keep your words in my journal and forever in my heart.

I could write about hundreds of people who carry our needs to the throne of God. Seeing their faces in my mind, along with writing about a few, brings me so much encouragement. We're not alone on this journey, and I'm reminded of this daily. I pray for you all, dear friends.

JUNE 6, 2017

I'm waiting on you, God. Not impatiently. I'm waiting to serve You. Waiting to fulfill Your plan. In Your infinite wisdom, You understand my confusion, and I know I heard You say, "Trust Me with all your days." I don't understand how such pain and my broken heart can be part of Your will, yet it is. You told me last December that if I trust You, really trust You, then all You are asking of me is to pray and believe.

Thy will be done.

JUNE 8, 2017

Tonight begins the first signs of terror dreams continuing into wake times. Jeanne and the doctors told me this would come.

We've slept in recliners in Larry's home office since November 2016. This way I can easily tell if Larry is sleeping or getting up. It also prevents Larry from falling out of bed.

During the night, he has a terror dream. When he wakes up, he walks into the kitchen and remains there for several minutes. I hear him walk from the kitchen into the living room, then back into the kitchen. I ask if he is okay and he softly replies that he's getting water. His balance seems stable, so I watch him move through the semi-dark.

When he returns to his office, he is obviously shaken.

We sit in silence for a few minutes. Then his voice cracks, as he gathers the strength to speak. "Please hold my hand," he says. "I'm so scared."

Whatever happened or whatever Larry thought happened terrifies him. I hold his hand and gently rub his shoulder. His entire body shakes. I silently pray for peace, clarity, and wisdom.

Larry goes in and out of sleep as I keep watch. Dawn is near, and I hope prayer and the light of day will begin to settle him.

Eventually, I ask if he wants to share why he was so upset

in the night. He says he heard the house alarm and someone breaking into the house. That he could hear them walking around, bumping into furniture. And although he could hear the intruders, he couldn't find who violated our sweet home.

"Honey, why didn't you wake me?" I ask.

"I didn't want you to be afraid or get hurt," he says. "I knew they planned to attack us. I hoped they didn't know where you were."

It took two days to recover from this delusional dream. Even in this delusional state, Larry Briggs, my husband of forty-six years, remains my hero.

Today is almost too difficult to face. *Stay steady*, I demand of myself. Maybe if I don't move, don't talk, don't journal, don't think, then maybe my lifeboat will stay afloat. Maybe I won't shipwreck. Maybe . . .

JUNE 10, 2017

Larry has always had a generous heart, but I need to find a way to keep him from paying for the meals of others when we are eating out. In two days, he's spent more than one hundred dollars on people he wants to bless. We've always done this, but not at this rate.

We're eating dinner out with friends, Janet and Maurice DeFord. Larry picks up the bill.

Maurice looks at him. "You don't have the money to pay for this," he jokes. Unfortunately, Larry lost his ability to joke months ago.

Larry shakes visibly, his face all fear. "I don't?" he asks me, his voice cracking. "We don't have any money in our account? Has our account been hacked or we just don't have any money?" He's overcome with panic.

We try to explain that all is well, that Maurice was pulling his leg. Larry nods that he understands, yet remains upset. Truth mixed with confusion.

JUNE 12, 2017: FATHER'S DAY WEEK

Larry doesn't recognize our city, the street to our house, or even the rooms within our house. He is in extreme pain, has no connection with reality today, and is barely able to move on his own.

Just when I think we are facing the worst day, today brings the harshest pain.

Along with Larry's medical challenges, we're facing a personal situation that is more heartbreaking than Lewy Body. To have someone we trusted take aim at our hearts is truly debilitating. Like Lewy Body, this person snuck into our lives and hurt my family. Now I'm forced to struggle with forgiveness while my head is already spinning. Desperately seeking strength, I silently repeat The Lord's Prayer:

Our Father who art in heaven, Hallowed be Thy Name.
Thy Kingdom come, Thy will be done,
on earth as it is in heaven.
Give us this day our daily bread.
Forgive us our debts as we forgive our debtors.
And lead us not into temptation, but deliver us from evil.
For Thine is the Kingdom, and the power,
and the glory forever. Amen.

The day I stood over my bathroom sink submitting to the will of God, I knew my Father in heaven was in control. His kingdom is not shaken by events here on earth. I'm secure knowing Larry and I are living out "Thy will be done on earth, as it is in heaven." I receive strength each day from His daily bread. I know when I come to the end of this challenge, God will receive all honor, power, and glory. I don't know how this will end, but I know God's plan for us is best.

However, I've not given thought to the middle of this prayer: "Forgive us our debts as we forgive our debtors. And lead us not into temptation, but deliver us from evil." I didn't see this part of The Lord's Prayer as having anything to do with the challenge we face.

I'm taken off guard. Unforgiveness stands so close to me today that I feel its hot breath. Forgive? I want to take this enemy on. I want to pay back pain with pain. I don't need back up. I can take care of this enemy alone. Before my unforgiving heart reaches a level of anger that I have not previously known, I'm reminded of God's word, "Forgive as I have forgiven you." I know, but God—right in the middle of this Lewy Body we have to face this new enemy and you want me to forgive? Immediately forgive? Forgive completely, the way You have forgiven me?

I go into the bathroom and lean over the sink where six months ago I asked God for strength to face the illness attacking Larry. Once again, I'm asking not why but what. What could it possibly take to turn this evil into glory for You? Once again, with a whisper to my heart, comes His same response. "Thy will be done. Give us this day our daily bread and forgive us our debts as we forgive our debtors." I feel too weak, too anguished, too spiritually inept to find the strength to forgive. I can't. Or maybe the honest answer is I won't. Yet He speaks gently to my breaking heart, reminding me of His unconditional, unfailing, forgiving love.

Lord, You forgive me immediately and completely, time after time. I don't deserve it either. I make a choice to honor and obey Your Word. It's not a matter of how I feel or even what I think. It's Your Word that is truth. I forgive. I trust You to help me forgive completely, relying on Your daily bread for the strength to do so.

This day is the first time I consider the advice given by UVA doctors and the support counselor. I reluctantly walk out the door to check on end-of-life care for Larry. I'm determined to only look at the facilities and plan to refuse any formal information. I just can't.

As I reach for the car keys, a phone call for help takes precedence. The emergency takes over my day, mind, heart, and every ounce of energy I can muster. Although the crisis has nothing to do with Larry's health, it stops me. I will not seek end-of-life care. It's not part of the plan.

JUNE 15, 2017

We need to leave for a few days. Clear our heads. Heal our hearts. Renew our thinking. We go to the beach and spend the weekend with Bryan and Kelly at Kill Devil Hills in North Carolina.

I love the beach, but this weekend is different. There is such immense hideous pain that I refuse to give it more life by recording it. Yet, it is just like our loving God to give us this blessing.

The condo is beautiful. The place we rented is overbooked, so they move us. We couldn't have afforded our new condo without this mistake made right by God. Kelly's mom, Vicki, is with us as well. She's a sweet, gentle person. Every time Larry sees her, he asks me, "Who's that?" Vicki overhears on occasion, but she's not flustered.

It's amazing that as lost as Larry is, he accepts that he's someplace he doesn't know and with people he doesn't know.

"I can tell they love you," he says often, "so I know it's

okay."

His trust is a blessing.

After telling him multiple times who Vicki is, Larry sadly says, "I should know her, right?"

I just remind him who she is and move on. It doesn't matter.

JUNE 18, 2017: FATHER'S DAY

Larry and I sit on the deck that looks out to the ocean. Beneath us is the pool. It's Sunday. I don't know if we've acknowledged it's Father's Day. None of us really care. We're together. The rest doesn't matter.

We just sit and enjoy the view on a gorgeous day. After about ten minutes, Larry comments on how beautiful everything is and asks several questions. I wonder if he knows it's Father's Day.

We watch the children play with their dads in the pool, while the moms relax in chairs or sit around the edge of the pool. Then Larry goes silent.

I sense the questions coming.

"Do you think those are good dads?"

I try to figure out where this is heading. I always keep my answers true, yet simple. No need to stir more confusion, more heart-wrenching questions. I say I don't know them, but they seem to enjoy being with their children, so yes, they are good dads.

Larry sits silently for several seconds, the cue that more questions are coming.

There is a deep sadness in his shaking voice as he ask, "Was I a good dad?" Tears fill his eyes.

"We were good parents," I say. "Not perfect, but we love our sons. You are a very good father."

I usually include myself in statements like this, hoping to take some of the load of responsibility from him. I don't know if it works or not, but it seems to help focus on us and not just him. I beg God, *Please let this be the end of questions related to family. Please, just not today.* But I don't get the answer I want. Instead, the uninvited visitor breaks down the door of my pleading heart.

"Did we ever bring the boys to the beach?"

The question plunges the burning spear deeper into my being. "Yes, you and I brought the boys to the beach almost every year."

I wonder how this evil illness can take that precious memory. My parents took my siblings and me when we were little. Then as adults, each sibling would pitch in and we'd rent a huge house and stay all week. After my dad passed away, we tried to keep the family tradition. It just wasn't the same, though, so it ended. But Larry and I continued as a family as often as we could afford. Having that memory evaporate is extremely painful.

Surely that's enough loss for the day. But Larry's not done yet.

"I don't remember that or anything about raising the boys."

There is no emotion to his words, which deepens the pain of my sobbing heart. One moment we're sitting outside with the ocean breeze gently blowing and the next all the air is vacuumed out! I can't breathe. We sit in silence for a long, painful time.

Is this another part of the long goodbye? I sink to a place I'd never felt before, yet more comes. How could there be more than forgetting the past with our sons? They are our world! I cling to the hope that family will always remain. I plead: *Please, I cannot take another blow. I can't.*

"How did I get so lucky to have you?"

The question is a tiny, tender moment—a moment just big enough to bring me a glimmer of hope. I reply that Larry is indeed a very lucky guy. It's not much, but it is all I can pull together.

Then even that brief moment dissolves as Larry adds without expression, "I mean, I don't remember us."

I force myself to breathe in and out. Isn't it supposed to be an involuntary response? If so, why do I have to remind myself to do it? Why? It's too much effort, but I must.

I scream silently, from a place so deep inside that words are useless and inadequate. I cry uncontrollably without a sound, without a tear.

So many events are happening—too many to record.

While Larry's disease progresses, his mind fails more each day.

All memories are gone. Ministry: Gone. Lifelong friends: Gone. Family memories: Gone.

There seems to be nothing left. Yet, there are the boys and their families. He has to look at their pictures and practice their names and who the grandchildren belong to, but he can do it. He doesn't have past memories of them, but at least he recognizes them. So, there is family. I'm thankful. It's enough.

JUNE 20, 2017

Our car is recalled. There is a serious problem with metal shavings from the ball bearings being thrust into the motor. I can't deal with this alone. Larry is having surgery in two days, and I have to decide what to do. We discuss the need for an SUV, as I am having difficulty maneuvering a walker and wheelchair into the trunk of our car.

I need Larry. I need him to be clear enough today to help me know what to do. Do we wait for the dealership to call us? They said we're on a long waiting list. I could try to find someone to fix our car after surgery or trade now for an SUV. The first two options will fall completely on me.

Larry is experiencing tremendous neck pain and his headache is excruciating. Surgery is in two days. We're hoping for relief. Larry insists he can help determine whether to fix our car or purchase a new one. He's strong even at his weakest point. I'm stressed making this financial decision. Is Larry really thinking clearly enough today? I decide to depend on him and trust God to lead us.

We search the car lot for hours, narrowing our decision. We begin the paperwork, but Larry is in such pain. I insist he go home to rest and tell the dealership we'll return in a few hours.

Larry falls asleep as soon as I get him in the car. Arriving home, he sleeps for another two hours. When he wakes, he insists he can continue, so we head back to the lot.

The paperwork takes too long. It's been over an hour. I can't do this to Larry. Somehow, I will figure it out later. As I stand to leave, the papers arrive. It's done. I have peace God led us to the correct decision, yet I feel weak thinking I should have been able to do this alone.

The truth is, I could have done it on my own. Truth? This may be the first of many life decisions I'll be making on my own, without Larry.

JUNE 21, 2017

Larry begins the morning saying he's going to call the insurance company to add the SUV. He puts the phone on speaker so I can hear and confirm the process. I'm trying desperately not to take all responsibilities from him, so we've agreed that business phone calls will be done together. He handles it well. He is so clear.

He hangs up the phone and puts the insurance information away.

"So, you bought a new car?" he asks innocently. "May I see it? May I sit inside? Do I get to sit behind the wheel?"

I watch from the garage door as he grips the wheel and pushes several buttons. He looks at me with excitement as he examines each feature. I force a smile through tears.

Each time he sees the car, Larry asks innocently, "Jane, did you buy a new car? I like the color. You did such a good job."

Each time, I cry.

JUNE 22, 2017

Today is Destiny's birthday. Our sweet, fun-loving granddaughter will be ten. Larry worries about missing her birthday party.

I have a love-hate relationship with the surgery that will be done on the last two discs in Larry's neck. They've put it off as long as possible. Dr. Mehta has performed five previous surgeries to deal with Larry's degenerative disc disease. The surgery was planned for January but was delayed until UVA's diagnosis was confirmed in May. The team decides now is the time.

Being put to sleep will likely further Larry's delusional state. He's at high risk of becoming combative, but I push the possibility so far away that it may as well be impossible. Yet, wisdom says beware. I decide that if Larry no longer knows me, I'll just say, "I'm the one God sent to take care of you."

No further explanation of who I am or who we are. It's a price I'm willing to pay if the surgery relieves him from pain. Letting him suffer with these continual headaches, while dealing with LBD, would be beyond unkind. The chance that at some point Larry would not understand this excruciating pain would bring me such heartbreak. I can't bare that possibility. My love for him will not allow it. It would be cruel.

Full of compassion, Dr. Mehta agrees to proceed with surgery in an effort to relieve Larry of his pain. He also wants to spare me of potential challenges by prolonging Larry's ability to make medical decisions on his own. We have total confidence in God's provision and Dr. Mehta's surgical skill. We are in good hands.

I know people are praying for us. I trust God's will for us. I feel numb but at peace. In three or four hours I'll see Larry. Until then, I'll just sit here and wait, writing out a few things about Juanita's visit from yesterday.

She drove to Virginia from Alabama just to see Larry before surgery, knowing this could be her last time to talk with him. It was Larry's best day in a long, long time. It was God's gift to Juanita, showing Larry's love for her. She's always been more like his sister than a cousin.

Larry was amazingly alert. He was concerned he wouldn't recognize her, so we studied her picture and reviewed some family facts. Not only did he know her, but he even pointed out her car in the motel parking lot. He asked her about a few family connections. We took Juanita, her daughter, and her granddaughter to dinner. It was almost perfect. Almost normal.

Earlier in the day, Larry spent a few hours with our precious friend, J.C. Cooper. They had breakfast together, got haircuts, and drove around. An all-around good day.

J.C. kept Larry active while I met with the support counselor, Taylor. It was difficult. I had to recount recent events and losses. She shared with me what is yet to come. Yet to come? How can they keep saying that? More? No! There can't be more! We're there!

As difficult as it is, I'm forever grateful. I felt an immediate connection with Taylor. She is professional, knowledgeable, and compassionate. I will be forever grateful for her wisdom. The sessions are painful because it confirms our situation is real. But I can't think about it today. I'll just focus on our time with Juanita. It was my reward that he had an almost normal day. I'll focus on that. For this moment, it's enough.

It's been several months now since we've slept in our bedroom. We moved into our home office in November 2016. The office has become our home. It's there we eat, sleep, review pictures, watch TV, think about not thinking. Our new normal.

Maybe I should sleep here in the waiting room while Larry's in surgery. After all, it's a chair like the one in the home office. But I can't. I'm beyond the need to sleep today, so I'll just write and stare blankly.

My writing and thoughts are broken by a nurse calling my name.

I'm prepared. I really am. Whatever happens it is His will for us.

The nurse walks me to the recovery room. I fear things aren't the best, but I already heard the surgery was successful. That's enough for now. I keep my eyes forward and walk, rehearsing my line if Larry doesn't know me: "God sent me here to take care of you." Simple truth.

The curtain is pulled back. Larry's face is blank. He

doesn't speak. I can't tell if he is here or not. The nurse says he's been very sweet. Not combative. That's enough for now.

Slowly, without making eye contact, Larry asks, "Jane, right?"

It doesn't shake me that he questions who I am.

"Yes," I reply.

He looks at the nurse. "Yes," he says, "this is the one I love."

The nurse smiles sweetly and assures me that he's been asking for his wife.

The disc surgery was successful. Larry has suffered with chronic headaches twenty-four seven for months, and now they're gone immediately! I'm beyond grateful.

Dr. Mehta has performed six surgeries on Larry for degenerative disc disease. He's more than just our neurosurgeon. He has become a compassionate friend. His care for Larry is amazing.

Today, there is one thing we can check off our list. Regardless of where God's plan takes us, pain will not be part of it.

Thank you, Dr. Mehta. I'm so grateful for the overwhelming, never-ending faithfulness of God.

JUNE 2017: THE LAST TWO WEEKS

The weeks of recovery following surgery are extremely painful for Larry, and medication eliminates only some of the pain. Gone, too, is more reality. I question why the pain goes away slowly while Larry's memory vanishes in an instant, without warning? Before surgery, we clung to glimpses of memory. Now, there isn't a single flash, not even a few seconds of clarity during the day.

"Is this our house? What's happening? Where am I? I

hear someone in the house. Are we alone? I was just talking to Robert. Where is he?"

Larry experiences additional dream terrors and balance issues increase dramatically. He's back on the walker, requiring constant assistance from me. I have a safety belt around his waist so I can secure him in my arms.

There are too many lost memories, confusion, and broken moments to record. I'll only journal one.

Larry is awake, so I ask if he wants me to turn on the lights. He doesn't answer. I hope he stays still and goes back to sleep, yet he continues to be restless—the signal that he is gathering strength to ask a question. I steel myself for what he may say.

Through a tearful, terrified voice he asks, "Where am I? Why am I in so much pain? What is wrapped around my neck? I can't move. What's happening to me? Who's here with us? I'm sure I hear someone."

I give a simple response. "We're home. It's just you and me. You're safe. You had surgery. The pain will stop soon."

How terrifying to wake up in the dark in pain, a huge, tight brace around your neck—not knowing what it is or why it's there.

I turn the lights on. He relaxes.

God is faithful in our time of need. I pray over Larry. He falls asleep for a few more minutes. We're both desperate for sleep.

Two weeks after surgery, the pain begins to subside. I'm so thankful to say goodbye to Larry's long-time physical pain.

The emotional and spiritual pain, unfortunately, continues. People stop by with food. I introduce friends as total strangers. I try to prepare them for the changes in Larry before they witness it for themselves, but it doesn't help.

It breaks my heart to see their faces as he says hello to them for the first time. To say I'm exhausted is an understatement. Our good days are those during which confusion is present, but the physical pain is gone. No more headaches. It's all that matters.

I only leave his side when I must. Today I think he's asleep, so I go to the kitchen to get the meal someone brought. I hear something in the hallway and find him clinging desperately to the walls, barely able to stand. I drop everything and run to catch him. He explains that he had come to get me to tell me he needs help getting up. It makes me dizzy.

I take him back to his chair and bring him dinner. I thought for those few seconds I could leave Larry alone. But I can't, even though he was sleeping! I'm so frustrated with myself. I'll have to plan better on when and how to walk into another room, even if only for a few minutes. Why can't I understand the okay moments are gone?

As I sit beside him gathering my thoughts, Larry becomes anxious. I ask if he needs anything.

"I need you to hold my hand," he says, looking down. "I'm scared."

I cry to God for help. He hears my cry and helps me think.

I turn off the lights, leaving only the soft sunlight pouring through the shutters.

I use my phone to play soft worship music and sit quietly, praying.

Larry asks me to cover him up. It is warm inside, so I ask if he is cold. "No," he says weakly.

He's not cold. He needs security and safety. I hold his hand. He trembles with anxiety. I cry and scream silently, a scream buried someplace so hidden in my inner being that not even I knew it existed.

This time, the tears race uncontrollably and wildly down my face into a pillow that captures my muffled gut moans. I push my face deeper and deeper into the pillow. I try to keep Larry from knowing I am crying, thankful he doesn't comprehend what he doesn't see. If he doesn't see me cry, he doesn't know I'm crying. I don't try to determine if that is good or not. I take it as a blessing. He doesn't see my pain and therefore doesn't know my pain.

Hours pass. The day passes. Night flows into morning. The days melt together. It may be two or three. I don't know. I don't care. It doesn't matter.

JULY 6, 2017

I can't bear the pain of today. "Thy Kingdom come, Thy will be done, on earth, as it is in heaven."

I hold my phone close to hear the words of "Do it Again" by Elevation Church. The church is located in Charlotte. That strangely comforts me. I'm from a small town forty miles southwest. The song normally makes me feel safe and close to my hometown of Clover. Close to family.

But today, I don't feel safe at all. I pull my body into a ball, cross my arms, and hold my shoulders, rocking and bringing comfort just as my dad did for me so many times. I tell myself, "You're safe, Jane. You're home. Climb onto the lap of your heavenly Father. He will hold you. You are His daughter." I press the phone tight to my ear so the words of the song block out everything else. My mind can't find words to pray. The lyrics pray for me. I know God accepts this song as my prayer of faith.

It is the only song I listen to now. It's my lifeline, my promise from Father that my walls will fall. Like Joshua, I'm walking around these walls of Lewy Body, waiting for them to tumble down. God directed Joshua to keep walking. God will cause the walls to fall only if Joshua obeys. God's promises still stand, not our walls. The wall of Lewy Body is too high, too sturdily built for me to take down, but my confidence is in God.

Nighttime is the hardest. Larry's limited abilities diminish even further when the sun sets. It's referred to as night-timers, when delusional symptoms are elevated. It is one reason the song is more precious to me: the symptoms are elevated. That's when Elevation's song takes me higher than my wall. It may be called night-timers, but these nights won't last.

My confidence is not in my ability to climb the wall but to climb onto the lap of my Father, because His word will come to pass. It's a hard lesson, but I'm learning the sweetest songs are sung from the praises of a broken heart. My heart is the vessel that houses the costly perfume of praise. When it breaks, the sacrifice rises from my tightly curled body to the throne of my Father. He gathers my costly praise and pulls its fragrance to His face, cherishing my broken offering. My Father has never failed me yet and He won't start now.

JULY 7, 2017

The night that follows is intertwined with nightmares. I pray they will not intrude into the day, parading as reality.

The same dream repeats time and time again. Larry dreams of my unfaithfulness. I don't want to know details. However, I can tell it is sickeningly cruel.

During the day, we talk about it only to confirm my love and commitment to him and to God. Our talks seem to help him keep it separate, yet every time he sees the man, Larry grows uncomfortable and upset. Jeanne told me Sam experienced the same symptom.

I refuse to journal anything we discuss. I don't want to remember it.

JULY 16, 2017

It's been almost five weeks since surgery. We haven't been able to attend church. Larry wants to go today. It amazes me how often he knows it's Sunday.

He seems physically stable, but unable to follow conversation. Although I know our days are not okay anymore, our daughter-in-law Amy and my beautiful grandchildren are here. With the additional family support, going to church is manageable. More than manageable. Larry and I desperately want to be in the house of God.

We go to the Chester campus to pray over someone. A few people greet Larry at his seat. He handles it well. No one knows Larry doesn't have a clue who they are or why they're talking to him.

Before getting to church, Larry and I worked out a system to make everything as smooth as possible. As someone approaches I say his or her name, and if I have time I'll tell Larry one quick fact about the person.

The first interaction is perfect.

"Hi Tammy," Larry says. "How's Rick?"

He says it so tenderly, I think my words connect him to the person, even if only for a moment.

He seems okay, perhaps enjoying a good moment.

Then the worship service begins.

"Where are we?" Larry asks, leaning toward me. "What kind of building is this? It sounds like a church."

My heart sinks. My throat constricts and I suddenly can't breathe. I scramble to organize short, simple answers. It's hard to determine the best response for Larry in a large crowd.

I begin wishing we hadn't come when Amy places her hand around my shoulder. Usually I don't respond well when someone touches me during a crisis. It makes me weak when I need to be strong. This time, it's different. Her touch is comforting, yet gives me strength.

Amy has helped me understand so many things during this time. In high school, she was hit by a drunk driver and suffered physically, mentally, and emotionally. Because of her accident, she has perspective that helps me understand moments that escape my comprehension.

Her hand still on my shoulder, I pull my thoughts together. "This is the school where Gracey, our granddaughter attends," I tell Larry. "We use it on Sunday for one of our church campuses."

I remain seated beside Larry as worship continues around us. I hold Larry's hand as he frantically scans the crowd behind us for anything—anyone—familiar. He's so confused that I can't get him to turn around in his chair.

Finally, the opportunity to calm him comes as our daughter-in-law Kelly sits in front of us. I point at her and whisper to Larry, "See, Kelly is here."

He says, "Yes," but the word doesn't mean he understands or agrees or is comforted by her presence. It means he hears me. Nothing else. He continues searching the crowd and seems suddenly relieved. "I know her," he says, pointing. "Rebecca." Hundreds of people are around him, including our family, and he knows Rebecca, the precious wife of one of our campus pastors. My hopes lift and my nerves relax somewhat as our son Bryan sits across the aisle from us. Adam, who serves as campus pastor, greets the people before Bryan preaches.

While Adam is still on the platform, I'm reminded why I can't let my guard down and relax. Too much risk, too many memories on the edge of loss.

"So is that man the pastor here?" Larry asks.

I feel a new depth of sickness.

"No," I say simply. "Adam helps Bryan. Bryan is the pastor."

As Bryan walks onto the stage, a new question takes aim at every fiber of my heart, soul, and mind. "So is that person Bryan? Is he the pastor?"

I nod and reluctantly surrender. The burning embers of gray ash have crossed the barrier of family, set it on fire, consumed us whole. Love of family is no longer the dividing line. Maybe it never was.

The tears gush down. It hits me like a bolt of lightning striking my head to my innermost being. I'm so weak. Everything goes black for a few seconds.

I realize I'm not crying alone. Larry cries, too. I wonder why and fear he either senses that he's confused or that my tears are upsetting him. I force myself to stop crying and ask if he wants to leave.

I begin wondering how I'll get him out of the building without causing total confusion. His arms and legs are shaking and limp at the same time. There is very little control. I hold his hand and rub his arms, desperate to bring peace and calm. I lean close and whisper, "Honey, I will take you home."

But he says, "No." He doesn't want to leave.

What faith! Who can endure being in a place with no idea what kind of place it is, who the people are surrounding him, and what he's doing here? Larry can. And he does.

I silently scream at myself, "There are no more okay

times! Get that into your head!"

Why do I let myself get tricked? I'm so frustrated with myself.

Bryan is in the midst of a series entitled "Tough Enough." Today's message is "Tough Enough to Stand." Larry seems to listen to every word. No matter what, he has always heard and received God's Word. He can no longer read, so I know God speaks to Larry spirit to spirit. It's enough. It's all that matters.

As Larry stares at Bryan, I'm thankful Bryan has no clue what the past hour has brought. Then I must remind myself to breathe when I realize I'll have to break the news to Bryan that Larry, his own father, doesn't know him.

I'm dwelling on this thought when Bryan takes me off guard.

"As most of you know, my dad is undergoing tremendous health issues." Bryan looks across the crowd and makes eye contact with Larry. "Dad," he says, "are you tough enough to stand?"

Larry shoots to his feet, answering Bryan's declaration of faith with a physical response. The people behind us gasp in response. Others applaud, whispering disbelief to one another. Larry hasn't stood by himself for weeks. Yet, he stands.

I grab the chair in front of me for stability as I stand beside him.

Yes, we're tough enough to stand.

"Give us this day our daily bread."

After church we have lunch together in Bryan's home. Larry is very weak. He needs help walking, help moving, help engaging in conversation. I prepare his plate. We eat quickly and go home. We don't discuss what happened at church. I don't tell Bryan that his father didn't recognize him.

Not today. Maybe never.

I get Larry home and to his chair. He sleeps for hours. I sit exhausted, but unable to sleep. I recall the scripture, "If I ascend to the highest heavens You are there. If I go to the darkest parts of the pit, You are there." (Psalm 139:8, NLT) My body and soul relax as the truth of these words penetrate more deeply than the painful shockwave experienced earlier.

Then I fall asleep in my recliner, too. It is well. It is well with our souls.

Days pass without writing. I've stopped posting dates when I do write. I don't know what day of the week it is. Those days I've not written contain the moments that are the most crushing, yet most cherished. I can't share them even with my own eyes. I can't bear to write. I can't take the chance of reading later what takes place in this, our sweet little retreat. I'll probably regret it, but for now the memories burn into my heart. Maybe I'll remember them later, maybe not. Today, I don't care.

JULY 30, 2017

Larry insists on going to the South Park campus today. This is Pastor Demetric and Tish's last day as our worship leaders, and Larry wants to join the staff in praying over them. I totally understand. Larry and I love Tish and Demetric. Telling them goodbye is important.

Unfortunately, the South Park campus is our largest and most difficult to enter facility. As soon as we enter, our good friend Ron Childs comes to our side. Pastor Kyle Montgomery joins the team effort as we maneuver Larry through the greeting crowd. We are blessed to see many friends we haven't seen for a while. Many reach out to hug and speak to us.

We greet them as best we can, while blocking Larry

between the three of us. I feel like the running back on a football field. I've got the ball. Ron skillfully blocks from the back, supporting Larry's inability to walk on his own, as superpower Kyle takes out people in front. The goal line is just ahead. Keep moving. Yes—touchdown! We made it to our seats. Might as well smile about it.

I insist we don't go to church that night. Larry needs to rest. But he wants to attend the going away party for Pastor Demetric and Tish after church. So we go. When we arrive at the restaurant, the crowd is more than expected. I suggest we say a quick goodbye and leave, but thoughtful Kyle saved us seats, so we sit.

Larry is somewhat blocked from the crowd and only a few people maneuver through the crowd to stop by to speak. I introduce each person to Larry. He says he knows each one, his normal response to avoid more confusion. Melinda Mutter is the last to stop by. I introduce her. Larry says he knows her. As Melinda walks away, Larry looks at me seriously. "I do know her," he says. "I know her husband, Aaron. He plays the guitar. We've known them for a long time. They used to attend our former church in Colonial Heights."

I'm taken off guard with this huge block of memory but dismiss it, expecting it to mutate into another moment when memory flashes back only to leave again. I've come not to trust those moments. I no longer allow my heart to be captured in the LBD trap.

Because of this difficulty trusting such moments, I'm totally unaware of the miracle knocking at the door.

Tonight, Larry tells me he plans to attend staff prayer Monday morning. I cautiously agree, but secretly think he'll forget. I wonder how he remembers there is a weekly staff prayer time at eight o'clock. I think of the next morning. If

Larry remembers and attends the prayer meeting, the staff understands to call or bring him home if Larry needs me. Larry insists he feels better, that he feels different. I watch as Larry chooses clothes for the morning meeting and sets them aside.

JULY 31, 2017

It's Monday morning, and Larry is showered, dressed, and ready to roll. I drive him to church and watch as he walks slowly, yet unassisted, to the door.

An hour and a half later, a staff member brings him home. Larry enters the house, saying he feels different. That he feels really good. That he wants to go to lunch, wash the car, and go shopping for new jeans. His to-do list is overwhelming. Shopping? That's been a big no-no for a long, long time.

He's determined to go to lunch. I agree, secretly deciding to see how things go and planning to react accordingly. He's had okay times in the past. He also went from needing no help to lots of help, from walking on his own to needing a walker and then a wheelchair. But today, for this moment, he seems clear-headed and his balance is good.

At lunch, he walks to the fountain and prepares our drinks. He carries both of them to the table without help. It doesn't register that he does this on his own. How I don't notice this amazing feat remains a mystery to me. I guess because normal is never normal.

Lunch is calm and peaceful. He talks about the staff prayer briefly and then changes the subject.

"Jane," he says, "this is a beautiful day. I want to go to the car wash and then go shopping."

I say nothing. Dismiss the comment. Know he won't remember this by the time we get to the car.

As we leave the restaurant, a police officer is waiting to order. Larry stops to thank him for his service. This isn't unusual. It will end with Larry paying for the officer's meal. I take a few steps toward the door, smiling to myself, hoping there's not more than one officer eating lunch here today. We can't afford the entire troop.

"I was a front-line chaplain for Chesterfield County for fourteen years."

My jaw hits the ground. Where did that come from? Larry hasn't acknowledged any past memories for over two months.

Larry pays for the meal. I don't help him use his debit card. I try to process what just happened as we walk to the car.

Larry opens my door before heading to the passenger side. I slide into the driver's seat and watch in the rearview mirror as Larry walks and opens his door. He slides in effortlessly.

I'm not sure what to think of these last five minutes. These things don't happen even on our best days. I don't allow myself to assume anything.

"Let's go wash the car," he says as he closes his door.

I consider asking him a question about the past. I think I'll ask about my family. Does he remember my siblings? He hasn't seen them in over a year. I'm considering how to phrase my question when Larry interrupts my thoughts.

"I want to call Bobby Hyne to ride along with him. He works in a relatively safe place now. That's a good place to start," Larry says, "if I want to go back to work with the police."

Larry married Bobby and Shannon years earlier. Bobby is a police officer and Shannon was my student teacher and then we taught together at North Elementary. When we visited them in their home two months ago, Larry didn't recognize them. How did he just pull that out of the air?

To this point, I have made a rule of not testing Larry with questions about what he remembers. However, this time I decide to break my rule.

I tell Larry I want to ask him a question from the past and if he knows the answer, that's great. If not, it doesn't matter. It's a strange, strained few minutes. I don't want to mess it up, so I proceed with caution.

"What can you tell me about my siblings?" I ask. "Here's a hint—there are seven of us."

Without hesitation, Larry names my siblings in birth order, their spouses, and a little fact about each.

"I know your dad passed away a long time ago," he adds. "And your mom—has it been one year or two? I'm not sure how long, but I know they are together in heaven."

The mention of my parents is a shock that brings tears to my eyes. I miss them desperately. Larry's correct, but I hesitate to ask or think more about it. It's way more than he's known since May, but what does it mean—or does it mean anything?

We head to the car wash, which is about fifteen miles away. We pass the street where our longtime friends Janet and Maurice live. We lived in an apartment about a block from their home for two years, the first time we lived in an apartment. We moved there to make house and yard maintenance easier after Larry's stroke five years ago.

Without my asking, Larry recounts that we've known Maurice and Janet for more than thirty years.

"I hope we helped them through the years as much as they have us," he says. "I enjoyed our adventure in apartment living down the street from them."

Encouraged by his comments, I press for more. I ask what he knows about churches, not including Destination, Bryan's church. I begin broadly.

"Where did you go to college and what did you do after that?"

He tells me where he went to college and then connects each church he has pastored, one after another. He declares his love for the churches. He hopes he helped them.

I don't ask any more questions. My thoughts are spinning so out of control I can't formulate a question. My mind can't take in what I'm hearing and seeing. Is this really happening or am I just so exhausted that I'm wishing this to be true? I'll just see where we go from here. At the moment, it's to the car wash.

Never has a car wash been so strangely exciting. I sit outside the station on a small stone bench, watching Larry take care of the details of getting the car washed. This is crazy! This is crazy good!

Do I dare venture out on the most difficult challenge for him and take him shopping? Do I dare take him on an activity we put away several months ago? The lights, the colors, the aisles; all of the people walking in different directions; the voices, the music, the movement—all of them triggers that bring on side effects of Parkinson's and seizures.

I decide to face the challenge.

Larry wants to go to a store about thirty minutes away. Maybe the drive will give me time to think and be wise about the whole thing.

We enter the store and I decide to walk away from Larry. He's not totally out of my sight, but I'm not by his side. He's not left the house alone since the disease set in, never wandered away, but am I pushing the boundaries? I am. And he proves that it's safe to do so—at least for today.

He shops for more than an hour and then wants to go to the next store. I move farther away from him, to the back of the store, completely out of sight. He shops for about half an hour, picks out the items he wants, and walks to the checkout line.

While Larry pays, I call Bryan to tell him what's happening. I think maybe if I say it out loud, tell someone who knows, they will be able to tell me what this means. I briefly share the events of the morning.

Bryan says in a hurried voice, "Good mom. I'm glad Dad is having a good day."

I start laughing before I end the call. Nothing is made clear to me. I know things aren't the same, but I don't know if this very good day is normal to someone going through the horrible illness. I'm not offended, sad, or disappointed by Bryan's response. I understand that I don't get it either.

Returning home, I expect Larry to sleep for an hour or two after such exertion. He doesn't. He is energetic and talkative to the point that he's overwhelming my ability to comprehend if what I'm seeing is real.

I'm so thankful for the day. I say nothing to anyone else about it. After all, I don't know what to say. Then day two, day three, and day four pass in the same way. Maybe I did misunderstand. Maybe I made this all up. Maybe it never really happened. I don't ask anyone if they ever heard of someone recovering from or overcoming Lewy Body Dementia with myoclonic seizures and Parkinson's. I hint to my sister that something wild is going on, but I am purposefully vague and unclear. I don't know how to put into words the unexplainable, the impossible.

Had Larry walked out on Monday, July 31, 2017, with Lewy Body and walked back restored? Did the miracle begin the night before at the going-away party for Pastor Demetric and Tish? Did it happen during the night while we slept? Wouldn't that be just like God? Did He perform the miracle while no one watched? Did it come quietly, unannounced? Did He cause my sleepy world to be a silent night, a holy night, all calm and all bright? Did Jesus gently appear while only angels stood guard? Did that precious Name announce the time has come for His will on earth as it is in heaven to be completed? He never told me how His plan would look nor how it would end.

I'd never heard of Lewy Body Dementia before Larry's diagnosis. It, too, had come unannounced. It came as a thief to kill, steal, and destroy.

However, I know another name: Jesus.

The name above all names.

The name that has come to set the captive free and heal the broken hearted.

The name to which every other name must bow and submit.

AUGUST 4, 2017

I'm meeting today with Taylor, my support counselor. On the way I prepare my thoughts, focusing on events since our last meeting in June.

Taylor and I met the day before Larry's disc surgery. We both shared our concerns about the possible combative effects surgery may have on Larry. How will I tell Taylor the horrific decline since I last saw her and of Larry's sudden, unexpected improvement?

Everything plummeted suddenly with Larry. Then again,

these are all the things she, along with doctors from UVA, prepared me to face. But surely she will have an opinion about these last four days. Will she have more insight? Will she say this is normal, that it sometimes happens, never happens, or that I'm not living in reality?

I'll just present the facts as they are. I know how to be factual. I've had plenty of practice, especially the last few months dealing with Larry. I'll give her examples of our good days, our not good days, and our indescribably horrible, very bad days that melt one into the next.

Seeing her at the door waiting to greet me weakens my entire body. Reminds me of how real these past six months have been. Yet, just seeing her brings me calm and clarity.

We walk into a small room at our local library and our session begins. I become tearful as I answer questions. Taylor asks me to indicate on a rating scale where we are on a daily basis. The session is so hard. Yes, Larry has lost expression in his eyes. Yes, everything about him is gone. Everything about us is gone. Everything you said would happen has happened. True, it's all gone. I can't bear the words coming from my mouth. I want to cover my ears, to scream so loudly I can't hear myself speaking. I want to believe all I'm saying and hearing are lies: horrible, vicious, cruel lies.

I know there's been a change, but it's so fresh. It's meaning is still unclear. Taylor's questions and my responses catapult me back to the reality of how real this is. Within seconds, I'm tossed from thinking *This isn't real, I'm making this all up*, to hearing Taylor's voice: "These are the things we've been preparing you to face." She's right. The doctors have been caring, honest, and truthful. I cry uncontrollably answering her questions.

I feel I'm caught up in one of those Hallmark movies.

Everything starts out beautiful. Then there's a horrific accident and a person loses all memory. The spouse tries everything to help bring them back, but nothing seems to work. Then in the last five minutes of the show . . . BAM! Everything turns out perfect.

My answers and her responses snap me back to reality. My brain is whiplashed violently back and forth: real, not real, real, no way, yes, no . . .

I continue to struggle emotionally as I respond to her questions although I know Larry is changed.

"This is what we've been telling you," Taylor reminds me. "You do have his name on a list for end-of-life care, right?"

I feel like one of my first-grade students who didn't do her homework.

I hesitantly respond, "No."

She sits up a little straighter.

I quickly continue. "No," I say, "but one day, when Larry was at the lowest point, I requested a friend to come care for Larry. I was walking out the door to look into end-of-life care when we got an emergency call. Someone desperately needed my help. I couldn't leave."

Taylor tries to say something, but I keep going.

"And I need to tell you about some changes."

I tell her about Larry coming home from the Monday morning staff meeting. Odd, but I relay the events of the past four days without emotion. I am factual. As if I'm totally detached from any personal connection. While I talk, I wonder how I can feel so detached, but keep talking.

Taylor barely moves. Her facial expressions give me no clue as to her thoughts. Her eyes are wide, but she doesn't indicate why. She continues with her six-page questionnaire rating scale. Her only comment: "Only answer these questions as it relates up to Sunday night, then we will discuss these past four days."

Upon completion of the rating scale, she closes her file and listens to me. She laughs slightly. "I can't write that down," she jokes, "or you'll get kicked out of the program." She's here to help me no matter the changes. She confirms she's never seen nor heard of such a recovery. "The MRIs, CAT scans, blood tests, cognitive testing, and doctors would all have to be wrong or you've had a miracle. Finding the tests and doctors all wrong will be highly unlikely."

Poor Taylor. I've had days to process this and she hears it all in a matter of minutes. She confirms our August 15 appointment with UVA Medical Center and leaves the interpretation of events up to them.

By the time I leave the library, I know Larry's sudden improvement is not normal. I continue to be thankful for each day's bread of provision and strength.

AUGUST 10, 2017

We are ten days into our miracle. Larry's thinking remains clear and his mobility is back to what it was before all this occurred. I discover he doesn't know about some events that happened during these past two and a half years. Today a friend asks Larry about the time he didn't recognize Bryan at church. Larry is shocked and upset. He insists he doesn't know what the friend is talking about.

I make a note to myself to be careful bringing up events until I learn what parts Larry recalls and what he doesn't. When something he doesn't remember is discussed, it brings him deep sadness.

I've learned he has no memory of us buying the SUV.

Now when he mentions the purchase, he laughs and says, "Yes, Jane, you did a good job buying us a new car." What once brought me to tears now causes us both to laugh.

As the days come and go, I learn of missing puzzle pieces that still don't fit. I'm so thankful Larry doesn't remember many of the events that still take my breath away. How precious of God to protect him from these things! My devotion for today is from Acts 9:33-35.

There Peter met a man named Aeneas, who had been paralyzed and bedridden for eight years. Peter said to him, "Aeneas, Jesus Christ heals you; get up and make your bed!" And he was healed instantly. Then the whole population of Lydda and Sharon turned to the Lord when they saw Aeneas walking around. (NLT)

I've never asked God why we had to walk down this difficult path. I only ask what God wants us to do. How do we take this situation and bring the most honor and glory to Him?

Aeneas' difficult path took eight years to complete, while ours was two and a half years. What we have in common is a long, difficult illness that took the ability to function normally. I don't know what caused Aeneas' sickness. I don't know what caused Larry's. I just know it came. Jesus said the same words to both men: "Get up and make your bed." The time of suffering and inability was over! Both men were instantly healed.

I have a new appreciation for the challenges of being instantly healed. It's amazing. It's miraculous. But it jerks your world around in a mind-boggling way. The important issue now is the last line of this portion of scripture: "Then the whole population of Lydda and Sharon turned to the Lord when they saw Aeneas walking around."

The healing was for Aeneas. The healing is for Larry and me. But the miracle is for those who turn to the Lord when they see Larry walking around. The miracle is for the church, the body of Christ, for each person with whom we are allowed to share our journey!

We haven't told anyone except family about Larry's healing. It is exciting to see the faces of those who saw Larry four days before. Just a few days before, he was unable to walk unassisted, had no memory, and looked lost and confused. Now he walks freely, chatting and smiling, checking up on how people are doing, asking about their extended family. It is nuts—simply, wonderfully nuts!

I can't explain every aspect of our miracle. Isn't that what a miracle is—the unexplainable? But I do know that this miracle didn't occur because of our name, what we've done or not done, who we are or who we're not, or that somehow we earned or deserved this miracle. We are weak, needy, and without Christ, helpless. We've done nothing more than attempt to follow our good Father's lead. Yet this I know and stand firmly upon: this level of pain and gain can't be without supernatural cause and effect.

I have no hidden agenda except to seek how this miracle can bring about the most glory to God. My heart's desire is to find a way to use our journey to cause everyone who comes in contact with our story to turn to the Lord.

As I write now, I wonder if this journal may offer someone else insight and hope. Perhaps it's just for our sons and their family. I don't know if anyone else would receive anything from reading it. My first thought is to send this journal to my daughter-in-law Grey and ask her to read it.

I feel God will give her direction and clarity.

···

AUGUST 13, 2017

Today is our forty-sixth anniversary.

Larry wants us to celebrate in Williamsburg, which is about forty minutes from our home. He's become the Energizer bunny. I think he's trying to make up for the two and a half years he lost. I'm all for it, but not in a few days. So I pushed against his idea of going.

Today is Sunday. In our forty-six years of marriage, we've never skipped church to go sightseeing and shopping. Someone in the church may notice the pastor is not behind the pulpit, but that's not the reason I'm hesitant. We are fourteen days into our miracle, and I'm still adjusting—struggling to adjust—to our drastic change. Instant healing isn't easy. That may sound strange, but it's true.

Some of the effects of this illness have impacted me in areas I never expected. Suddenly, I'm not confident driving to new places, yet I'm required to do it often. What should be simple decisions become big challenges. Do we go to Williamsburg or not? I can't decide. But it's more than that. I want life to stay calm. Don't want to interrupt our miracle. Don't want to rock the boat even the slightest. I'm walking on water and there is no boat waiting in the distance.

I finally agree to celebrate by spending the day in Williamsburg. What woman doesn't like the idea of shopping the Williamsburg Outlets? The drive is easy. Relaxing even. I'm quietly proud of myself. We shop for about two hours, staying together some of the time, shopping separately at other times. It is wonderfully uncomfortable and feels oddly risky. I glance around for Larry. Text to check on him. This is no longer a test for his recovery, but mine. I decide to pass the test with high marks by pushing those fearful thoughts aside and enjoying the day as if the past year had not happened.

Our day is peaceful, uneventful, perfect. We stroll the outlet mall like a normal couple, enjoying this shining beacon to shoe lovers. I follow the hypnotizing light and add a pair of beautiful sandals to my growing collection.

AUGUST 15, 2017

We're at UVA Medical Center. The appointment was made on May 5 during our last visit, the day we received the official diagnosis of Lewy Body, the day we were given two weeks to get end-of-life decisions made. What an unspeakably difficult day that was.

I don't think Dr. Barrett expects us to show up for our appointment. I'm positive they don't expect what we are bringing for show and tell. I remind myself that it doesn't matter what they say. Their report doesn't change what is happening. We are fifteen days into our miracle.

Will the doctors be like so many well-meaning friends who have cautioned me not to expect too much, that things could change, that I should just be thankful for these few good days? Often people enduring such devastating illness improve just days before...well, before everything ends.

Good days? I've lived this twenty-four seven. I know the difference between what is happening now and what I called our good days. Our good days were not full days. There were hour-by-hour changes. Sometimes, minute-by-minute. A good day could go the other way in the blink of an eye.

I know our friends' words of caution are spoken from hearts of love and concern. But unless you are the caregiver, you cannot understand. I'm thankful they don't. I hope they never experience anything close to this.

As we sit in the waiting room, Larry and I formulate a plan. I will confirm the past few months much like I did with the support counselor: the loss, the struggles, the bad days, and the horrific days. Then we will tell Dr. Barrett about the past fifteen days.

The doctor walks in and glances around the room. When he sees our son Bryan, me, and especially Larry, he's a little taken back. He stops in the doorway.

I take a deep breath to begin our explanation. Before I get out the first syllable, Larry announces, "Well, God healed me!"

Typical Larry—there goes the plan!

As Dr. Barrett carefully takes a seat, I confirm the events of the past three months, events that occurred just as Drs. Brown and Barrett said they would. But then Monday, July 31, came and Larry attended staff prayer at church.

Dr. Barrett sits calmly, stunned, processing and struggling to accept the change—the change he sees for himself.

"Let's see you walk down the hall," he says after some thought. "It's not the exam I planned, but let's see if you can do it."

Dr. Barrett starts toward the exam table, hand extended to help Larry down, when Larry hops down on his own. Dr. Barrett yanks his hand back. Freezes in his tracks. Stares in disbelief for an awkward moment. It's his first clue that a huge change has taken place.

I follow to the doorway. Larry walks past three exam room doorways, turns, and walks back—feats he couldn't perform without great effort at our last appointment. At the May visit, it took effort to take just a few steps unassisted. Larry couldn't turn or step backward without losing his balance. What a difference!

As they return to the exam room, Dr. Barrett keeps his eyes on Larry. "Where do you guys go to church?" he asks.

We give a few quick elevator speech explanations. One church, three campus . . . where you're going matters. We spit out a very abbreviated focus statement. And I'm pretty sure we never even said the name of the church.

We sit looking at each other and then back to the doctor, waiting for his response.

Dr. Barrett folds his arms across his chest. He smiles, accepting what has obviously happened outside the realm of medicine. Says he needs to process a few thoughts as he scans the computer list of medications and tests.

"Oh, well," he says, "we didn't have time to give you anything and the meds you are taking wouldn't affect LBD."

He clarifies that UVA Medical Center didn't have time to offer therapy nor medication due to the advanced stage of Larry's disease and his concern over the effects of being put to sleep from the disc surgery in June. The August 15 appointment was set to see if anything else could be offered, depending on Larry's status. And Larry was already past the May 19 timeline.

The doctor continues to listen to our review of the past fifteen days. It is a rather short appointment.

The three of us get into the elevator to head to the exit. We stare at each other, looking for assurance that we all just heard the same report. That it's done. Over. Official.

Larry is healed.

Today is a different ride home from that of May 5. Oddly, it's still overwhelming, and both days seem unreal. I want to roll down the car windows and shout with unspeakable joy the good news that Jesus is still in the healing business. Yet I silently ask myself, *Did any of this really happen?*

But as for me, I trust in You, Lord;
I say You are my God.
My times are in Your Hands.

—Psalm 31:15

Photo: Ivy Briggs

REFLECTIONS

As I begin to understand LBD, I recognize the misdiagnosis from the past two years, which began to manifest in July 2015. Doctors thought the attacks were TIAs, mini strokes. Sometimes they thought Larry was experiencing a reaction to medication. No matter what changes they suggested, nothing ever stopped the spinning cycle. On and on came the attacks.

I look back and see why I misunderstood statements and out-of-character actions from Larry. He would say things to me that broke my heart, yet later didn't acknowledge what was said. He would look at me as if I was telling him things about someone else. None of it was like him, yet I couldn't fathom what was going on.

They were the most confusing, painful months of our forty-six years of marriage. It wasn't him. It wasn't us. And I know now it was the beginning of this long goodbye.

Was the long goodbye to be a farewell to our past? Was it a long goodbye to Larry's ability to walk, feed himself, function independently? Was it a long goodbye to him?

I didn't know. But if that was part of God's plan, then He would provide. Our Father would provide either way. After all, He's more than enough. He's never failed me and He won't start now.

AUGUST 20, 2017

Today marks twenty-one days into Larry's healing. Bryan wants to keep it quiet. He wants to wait three days to announce it to the church leadership at the soft opening of the new building. Then he will share it again on Sunday with the entire church.

However, the secret is leaking out. Anyone who speaks to Larry recognizes the change. I love seeing their eyes when they do. As Larry walks away from speaking to people, I answer their shocked expressions that "Yes, we are having a very good day."

I tell a few people when asked, but I'm learning to pull back. Those I thought would understand a miracle simply don't.

"It's good God is giving you a few good days, but don't get your hopes up."

"I know someone who had something like that and it came back."

"I don't want it to be too hard on you when it returns."

They mean well, and it doesn't upset me. In difficult times, we think we need to say something and when we do, it often doesn't help. Besides, I've already been to the place of Too Hard. Too Hard was taking pain-filled nauseating sips of a bitter, burning drink as I planned for Larry's end-of-life care, how he wanted this or that to be taken care of. I can't write those things in my journal. I keep them in a separate little notebook I called "Issues." It's here I placed our will, advance directive, numbers, bills, what to do if he worsens, if he . . .

Yes, I've already walked to and through the place of Too Hard, and my heart aches for those still on that path.

SEPTEMBER 2017

I know the healing is for us, but the miracle is for others.

Grey has finished reading my journal. She and I determine we are too emotionally involved to read objectively, edit, or decide if it has value for others. Grey has asked a friend, Daniel Brantley, to read it and offer his opinion. He's agreed. Our family met Daniel when we moved to Chattanooga. He was in the tenth grade with our youngest son, Robert. I lovingly refer to Daniel as my favorite son. What a joy that he's now an editor and author.

Daniel's thoughts will determine the direction of this journal. Is it possible that our journey through this horrific illness can be an encouragement to others? What part of this miracle can be used to turn people to the Lord? I have total confidence in his decisions not only because of his amazing talent, but also because God chose him. He chose Daniel to offer editorial advice and wisdom in determining direction.

With great peace, I hand my journal to Daniel. It's a tangled mess of emotions and thoughts, strands of hopes and fears. It displays our days of strength as well as weakness. It's our journey of walking through the Valley of the Shadow of Death to the table spread before us, the miracle God gave so that others would marvel at His glory. Surely goodness and mercy has chased us down, overtaken us, blessed us beyond measure. All this I've tasked Daniel with untangling like a skillful weaver. It's our simple true story, but Daniel's skill will produce a tapestry of grace, mercy, and love. I know him. He will not look for earthly credit, but heaven takes note of all the fruit that will be produced by his pruning.

OCTOBER 5, 2017

Larry and I are going out to lunch today with our friends, Jim and Diane Fleshman. Jim is one of four men whom I depended on to care for Larry when I had to take care of business. It was important for Larry to stay in contact with these trustworthy men and I needed to know that Larry was physically safe with men who understood Larry's confusion and struggle.

There were other dependable men, but I had to keep Larry in direct contact with the fewest people possible, especially when leaving him. It took a long time to rehearse who was coming to be with him. Fewer people made it easier for Larry to connect who they were. Larry usually did well for those short periods of time, even enjoying his time with them.

Now, it's such a joy to go to lunch with friends. It feels so normal, so safe.

While we wait for them to arrive at our house, Larry asks to read my journal. I'm not sure he remembers that I kept one over the past year. I hesitate, unsure if it is best for him. I never planned on anyone reading it. However, I agree. Then I walk out of the room and leave him with the secrets of my heart.

I walk by the room several times to see if Larry's okay. It reminds me of the many walk-by checks from the days of so much hurt and pain.

He seems interested, yet looks as if he's reading the newspaper. I wonder why he's not bothered by the journal, but I am thankful. He stops, shuts the journal, and closes his eyes.

"Are you okay, Larry? Do you need to stop?"

He doesn't answer right away. Takes a deep breath before saying he's okay. Explains that he just needs to think about what he read. A few moments later, he starts reading again.

Finished, he closes my notes.

"So," I say, "does it bother you to read this?"

"It doesn't bother me in the least." He speaks clearly, calmly. "I'm just glad I'm healed."

Handing me the journal, he stands and faces me. He says he doesn't remember any of the events in my journal.

"It's like reading a heartbreaking story about someone I don't know, except I'm in the center of the story." Larry chokes back tears, yet forces himself to continue. "I can't believe you went through all that for me."

After months of carrying a heart of grief that Larry went through so much, he stands here feeling sorry for me. How can this be?

I tear up with mixed thoughts. I'm struck with loneliness, knowing we went through this horrendous illness and can't share its moments together. We've always faced life's challenges as a couple. Then I move from grief to relief and then joy, as I rejoice that God shielded Larry from the pain and misery of the last year—another gift we do not deserve!

Larry doesn't have to remember the painful losses. The gray ashes that once lay in a pile at my feet have been raised to new life. My friend Beverly Balint said it best in a text. She wrote, "The Spirit that raised Christ from the dead has brought Larry back from the ashes of defeat, the resurrected King has resurrected him." I'm overwhelmed with the goodness of God.

At this point I figure anything is possible, so I ask Larry if he'd like to add his thoughts to my journal. What did he experience? What does he remember? How did he feel?

...

OCTOBER 23, 2017: LARRY'S REFLECTIONS

Reading Jane's journal has been very difficult, yet unbelievingly confirming. I've always said she's the greatest gift God has ever given me. Understanding how hard these past two and a half years have been on her is heartbreaking, yet it deepens my love and appreciation for her—if that is possible.

I have very vague memories of the past two and a half years. Some memories are clearer than others, but most get lost in a fog. I have a clouded recollection of being tested and the process of losing my memory and mobility. However, from November 2016 until my healing on July 31, 2017, most of life is a blended blur.

The horrid feeling of not knowing who I was, not knowing those around me, was strong. Perhaps the hardest time for me was sitting in church. For a brief moment everything was clear. Then without notice, I didn't know anything: where I was, who was around me, whether the person I was talking with was a stranger or family. It was terrifying. I can only imagine how frightening it was for Jane and our family. I'm so deeply thankful for their strong love, faith, and support.

One lesson we have all learned is to never give up. God's thoughts are not our thoughts, and neither is His timing always in line with ours. And while we cannot know His timing, we do know that He is always in control of everything that touches our lives.

I cannot find adequate words to express how wonderful it is to be back. Honestly, it is like I went to sleep one night and woke up two and a half years later. I think our friend Aaron Mutter said it best: "Pastor Larry, it's like you have come back from the dead." I couldn't agree more.

Despite the chaos and confusion, I remember clearly the presence of God throughout this ordeal. Daily I was aware of His nearness. I'm not sure when, but at some point during my battle with LBD, it became a struggle to read. Letters became jumbled swirls of ink marks, and I was left without the ability to study His Word. I had read the Bible in its entirety several times per year, and I'm thankful I did, as that enabled me to keep His Word hidden in my heart.

Through Jane's constant care and presence, I knew He was with us. I experienced times of unimaginable fear, accompanied by shattering anxiety from not understanding what was happening. Yet I always had His comfort and was aware He was deeply involved in all of this.

On Sunday evening, July 30, I began feeling better. There was no thunder. No lightning. Rather, I felt an overwhelming sense of peace. The night of Pastor Demetric's farewell dinner, I began to recognize people. When Melinda Mutter placed her hand on my shoulder and said she and Aaron were praying for me, I knew her and remembered that she and Aaron were dear friends whom we had known for many years.

When I woke up on Monday, July 31, everything was normal. I knew I had staff prayer and devotions at eight that morning, so I started to get ready. My only confusion was why I couldn't drive, but I trusted Jane. I knew she had my best interest at heart, so I said nothing and let her drive me to church for staff prayer. As I entered the door of the church, I turned and watched her drive away. I wondered why she drove me and why this morning was different.

Since then, I've felt better with each passing day. On August 4, I told Jane that God had completely healed me. We are now four months into this miracle and I feel better than I have in years.

Recently, I preached at Matoaca Christian Fellowship for Pastor Ryan Atchison. In a few weeks, I'll speak at our home church, Destination. I'm also scheduled to speak at Life Church in Colonial Heights where Jane and I pastored for years. Their current pastor, Scott Tischler, is a precious friend. I mention this because sharing God's Word is one of my greatest joys. It confirms my healing.

To all our faithful friends who prayed earnestly and consistently for us throughout this journey, thank you. To the few men who got past Jane's interview for gatekeeper, thank you for being willing to sit and watch over me. I'm eternally indebted to you. Jane and I acknowledge that serving God and His church has been a tremendous blessing and honor. One of the rewards is having great faithful friends who carried us to the rooftop and brought us to the feet of Jesus for healing. We love and appreciate each of you beyond words.

The questions Jane and I have now do not revolve around why we had to walk through this very dark place, but rather what God's purpose is in it all. How will He use this for His glory? We both firmly believe the healing was not just ours but more so for His Church. We live in critical times during which people need to know our Heavenly Father deeply loves and cares for each of us.

Coming out of this, God has spoken some personal and powerful truths to my heart. I will share them as He directs in His timing. For now, let these words suffice: there has never been and never will be a time when He is not in total control.

Psalm 31:14–15: "But as for me, I trust in You, Oh Lord; I say You are my God. My times are in your hands." (NASB)

...

OCTOBER 25, 2017

How immensely gracious of God that Larry doesn't re-member most of the past two and a half years. His steadfast trust in God and our marriage during our darkest moments are a reflection of the Father's love, which doesn't diminish with trails, but only deepens and becomes richer.

I hesitate to reveal this part of my journal, this sacred moment between God and me. However, I'm willing to risk it all for the possibility that it will encourage others to draw strength and peace knowing that—as Larry has shared—our times are in God's hands.

When I saw that Larry closed with that scripture in his journal entry, I knew it was time to share God's kindness in preparing me for what was coming—the long goodbye. So I'm sharing what I painfully disclosed with our three sons and their precious wives on that hot May afternoon in our family meeting: How God prepared me for what we were about to face.

On Christmas morning 2016, God entrusted me with His plan. That's right, it didn't start on May 5, when we received the Lewy Body diagnosis. It began five months earlier.

Larry had become different. Through the years, he has been consistently caring, thoughtful, and calm no matter what. He always thinks of others first and puts himself last. Not out of false humility, but because he genuinely hungers for others' good. He has always been willing to suffer loss if it means gain to someone else—especially the church body. All that changed over the duration of his illness. Larry spoke harsh words and lacked emotions. Making it worse was that he was unaware how these changes impacted me. I was so confused and completely unaware of the reason for such dra-matic changes.

I won't share some of the most painful moments, but one will illustrate the change. We were at lunch one Sunday with Bryan, Kelly, and their four sweet children, when out of the blue Larry made an announcement for all to hear. "I have no emotions," he said flatly, "and I don't care about anyone or anything. Things and people are distant to me. It's like you are all far, far away."

I tried to cover for him, to soften the blow for Bryan, Kelly, and the grandchildren. But nothing I said could bring Larry around, so I left it there. He had said similar, harsher things to me, but this was the first time he spoke it to family. They were gracious and said nothing.

That small glimpse should help you understand Christmas morning 2016. It was dismissed as a dull, unimportant day. Larry didn't even acknowledge it was Christmas.

Late in the day, we were going to watch Bryan's family open their Christmas presents, but Larry said he didn't care if we went or not. My heart couldn't comprehend his words.

I tried not to be discouraged or think of all our beautiful memories of Christmases past, but I was crushed. Then God gave me direction—soft, clear direction. It felt odd, but I did what He said. I turned on "Unchained Melody." I knew the song, but Larry and I had never danced or claimed a song to be "our song," so we had no history with the tune or any other song. Not in that way at least. We pastored during a time when that was not acceptable. Dancing with your spouse was…frowned upon.

Because we never danced together, it made the situation awkward. I invited Larry to join me in the living room near our Christmas tree. I knew he might reject the invitation. He was compliant, but uninvolved. As we danced, I felt so painfully alone. I didn't want to obey God's instructions, but I went beyond myself to do as He asked. I wrapped my arms around Larry's shoulders. He barely moved, but I obeyed God's voice and waited to see what to do next, if anything.

To my surprise, God tenderly delivered this message to my waiting heart: "This will be your last Christmas with Larry as he is today."

I didn't seek its meaning. I refused to let my thoughts wander to all the what ifs. However, I knew it was a warning of more difficult days to come. I accepted that God was in control and whatever that meant, I'd not ask for more.

"I'll follow Your plan," I whispered to God. "I trust You. Our days are in Your hands."

I cried as I leaned against Larry's shoulder. He didn't respond, and the song ended.

"Here," he said, "I want you to go ahead and open your gift."

He had ordered a gold heart necklace with our names engraved in silver. I wondered in what brief moment of clarity he placed the order. The thought faded, as I had witnessed such moments before.

Larry's words gave me a glimmer of hope that today would be more like Christmases past. However, he remained distant. With nothing more said, he turned and walked out, returning to our home office. I was left standing there, just as I'd been before he entered the room and while he was there: alone. I held the gift he gave me. It seemed a paradox now: a heart with both our names intertwined on it, while my heart was crushed with total abandonment. I thought it impossible to feel less connected to him.

Alone but held firmly by God's arms, I whispered to my Heavenly Father, "As for me, I will trust in You, Oh Lord. I say You are my God. My times are in Your hands."

NOVEMBER 18, 2017

I've never put our Christmas tree up this early. A year ago, I didn't understand that November marked our last six months together.

Larry and I stand together, gifts wrapped and under the tree, enjoying the lighting of the tree. Larry is excited to celebrate, unencumbered by any memory of last year's holidays.

The tree looks more beautiful than ever. We look at it through new eyes. Eyes that have witnessed and personally experienced a miracle.

DECEMBER 25, 2017: CHRISTMAS

I don't know what our tomorrows will bring, but I know God holds each one in the palm of His hands. I'll continue to learn to trust Him more.

Today, we stand in front of our tree. We hold each other, more in love with God and each other than ever before. The presents remain wrapped under our beautiful tree. Though they are carefully wrapped and purchased with love, the contents can't compare to the gift God has given us in His Son.

Larry and I stand hand in hand, overwhelmed by God's goodness to us. We know He didn't have to grant Larry's health, but we bask in the amazing generosity of this miraculous healing. We hold each other tightly as we dance to "Unchained Melody"—our song.

We have come full circle.

We rejoice in Jesus, the reason for our season, and celebrate the end of The Long Goodbye.

EPILOGUE

It was Memorial Day weekend when we told my two brothers and their families that Dad had been diagnosed with Lewy Body Dementia, a life-altering and life-ending disease.

Memorial Day started normal enough. We grilled out as all ten grandchildren enjoyed the outdoors. Then the moment came.

We broke the news, cried together, and comforted each other, unsure what the future held for our family. But one thing we were sure of was who holds our future. If there was one message that Mom and Dad passed on to us, it was that no matter how uncertain life seems, there is one constant: our faithful God. We were raised knowing and believing that with God all things are possible and that He can turn any situation around for our good. We knew the same Spirit that raised Christ from the dead lives in us and can raise us out of any difficult situation in which we find ourselves. We have seen Mom and Dad teach and—more importantly—live this message our entire lives. We knew this illness wouldn't stop any of us from believing for our dad's healing miracle, because we know God loves to do what others say cannot be done, and He does this so He can receive all glory and that people might believe! We also know that unless our faith is tested we will never have a testimony.

Everyone wants a miracle, but few want to need one. Well, we needed one. So we trusted God and believed that regardless of the outcome of Dad's illness, he would be healed—either in this life or the life to come.

Mom's account encourages you to cling to your faith when everything you love is slipping through your fingers. You also witness the miracle that we all believed God for, a miracle that will inspire and encourage you to believe. If God can do it for our family, He most certainly can do it for yours.

Bryan Briggs
Lead Pastor of Destination Church
Hopewell, Virginia

MORE FROM SIR BRODY BOOKS

Christian Inspiration

ANTICIPATING THE UNEXPECTED: LIVING A BLESSED LIFE
LEIGH ANN COATS

We all yearn for something more—peace, fulfillment, blessing, and a deeper relationship with God. By actively seeking God and anticipating the unexpected ways He works in the details of our lives, we can discover the unlimited and all-sufficient beauty of God's blessings to all who are in Christ. Walking with God, living in Christ, and following the guidance of the Holy Spirit—this becomes the adventure of a lifetime!

Children's Fiction

I'M 12 YEARS OLD AND I SAVED THE WORLD
D.K. BRANTLEY

I'm Adam—Adam Shannon Dakota Carr. Yeah, it's a terrible name. But it gets worse. I've got a super lame cell phone and Mom won't let me cut my hair. As if things aren't bad enough, Dad loses his job and Mom and Dad's marriage is on the rocks. Now it's up to me to fix everything. That's right—I'm 12 years old, and I'm about to save the world.

Made in the USA
Middletown, DE
05 August 2020